Vision
is
Victory

Vision
is
Victory

Where *Hopes* and *Dreams* Become *Action* and *Achievement*

Carey Conley

LaCoCa Press
Greenwood Village, CO

Vision is Victory: Where Hopes and Dreams Become Action and Achievement
Published by LaCoca Press
Denver, CO

Library of Congress Control Number: 2015949069

Conley, Carey Author
Vision is Victory: Where Hopes and Dreams Become Action and Achievement
Carey Conley

ISBN: 978-0-9966999-1-4

BUSINESS / Consulting
BUSINESS / Entrepreneurship

QUANTITY PURCHASES: Schools, companies, professional groups, clubs, and other organizations may qualify for special terms when ordering quantities of this title. For information, email the author directly at Carey@CareyConley.com.

LaCoCa Press

Dedication

This book is dedicated to my sweet, amazing God,
who gave me the clarity of purpose in helping others
find their vision and gives me the strength to carry
out my mission here on earth every day.

And to my children, Cole and Laurel, who continue
to be the wind beneath my wings.
You were my why from the moment I envisioned you both.

Contents

Introduction

Imagine yourself eating an ice cream cone—one of those waffle cones that come to a point at the end—filled with one scoop of your favorite flavor. Now visualize yourself attempting to eat that ice cream cone from the bottom up. The kid in you may think this would be a lot of fun. In actuality, though, you'll soon discover that it's almost impossible to keep up with the ice cream as it drips out from the bottom, especially as you work your way up the cone, where the opening becomes bigger at the top. The reality is that eating an ice cream this way creates a big, sticky mess. Before you know it, you've got ice cream dripping down your hands and arms, and even your chin.

This may seem like a comical scenario to envision, but believe

∞

it or not, this is how most of us run our lives and our careers. We bite away at the tip of our daily "to-do" lists without any idea of the desired end result we are moving towards. We try to make our daily activities work in the direction of a goal, but oftentimes those activities have no relationship to a clear vision. Most of the time, we don't have a true picture of exactly where we're heading. By the time we get to what we thought was the grand reward, we find that we've ended up somewhere we don't even feel good about. Our concept of the reward we were moving towards has dripped away, if it was ever there in the first place. All of the daily effort we've put in makes us feel productive in the midst of completing each task, but when we reach "the end," we may be left with a sense of emptiness, uncertainty, and dissatisfaction. We may even feel lost.

Many years ago, I found myself in that very place. I was following a "normal" life path, the same path most people I knew were also taking. Just as most everyone did after high school, I earned a college degree in business—a major feat because I had not been a great student. I married my high school sweetheart, moved back home to Colorado after college, and went to work in the corporate world, along with the rest of our tribe. It was the early eighties and we were all doing the same thing—putting all of our efforts into climbing the ladder of success.

I changed jobs every two years because I wasn't happy. At

∞

each job, I didn't seem to fit the mold. So, when everyone else was moving up, I was moving on to find that one job where I would fit. I believed there was something wrong with me—that there was something lacking in me.

At job number three, I was blessed to hear and meet a speaker who became my mentor and the very first person who told me I was never going to fit into the corporate mold. She told me I needed to find a different path. After the initial shock of her words, it became clear that there was nothing wrong with me. I simply needed to find the thing I was passionate about and build a business around it.

She introduced me to a book written in the early eighties, *How to Get Control of Your Time and Your Life* by Alan Lakein. This led me to decide it was time to focus in and look at what I really wanted for myself. I took a day off from my job so I could spend the day looking inward. I got a yellow legal pad and began to write. I wrote down the specifics of what I wanted my life to look like. I included everything: my husband, our marriage, where we would live, our future children, my values, and who I wanted to be professionally one day in the near future. Waving my magic wand, I saw myself running a company that empowered women. I wrote down that I wanted to work in skin care or in health and wellness. I wrote that I wanted to be a speaker on stage—showing people how to create their vision and set goals around it. This

∞

was 1988. I knew what I wanted but I had no idea how it would happen.

Amazingly, everything I wrote down began to occur. It was the ripple effect of one thing leading to another. I felt very connected to God as things began to unfold. After the birth of our son, while still working full-time, I was invited by a friend to an Arbonne party. I learned about the possibility of working from home, of having a flexible work schedule and the opportunity to earn residual income. After the birth of our daughter, I began moving up within Arbonne. In three months' time, I'd moved to the first level. From there I continued to move up the ladder and in the process learned that I loved to coach other leaders on their vision and their why. I helped them look at their "without air to breathe" vision—that vision that was so essential to their being they couldn't help but be successful. Without such a vision, it is easy to quit and give up.

A few years ago, after my daughter left for college, I began coaching outside of Arbonne. I started by beta testing five people, including one friend who worked with me remotely. I used a six-week course I'd developed. It proved to be a huge success. After six weeks, each individual had a clear vision and very specific plan. I continued to coach more people and then developed a one-day workshop, where thirty to fifty people participated together. At the end of the day, each person would walk out with that same clear vision and specific plan. Today, I continue to offer a one-day "Vision is Victory" workshop. I also take the stage whenever possible to inspire others and help them create their vision and set goals. Looking back at that yellow pad of paper, I see that everything I envisioned has become reality. It took only one day of visioning to create the amazing life I now lead and that I have the privilege to share with others each and every day!

I hold the belief that God gave each of us a very specific assignment to achieve while we are on this earth. Imagine that he stuck a note in your pocket before sending you down here to "school." The note is His voice telling you what you are here to do and why you are living at this particular moment in time.

Each of us as children was an authentic individual. It wasn't something we worked at being—we just were. Sometime around middle school (junior high for some people), we began to take on the programming that was imposed upon us. We stopped connecting with our inner selves and instead began to focus on outer influences. Those influences came by way of parents, school, community advisors, and even friends. Before we knew it, most of us had lost touch with who and what we truly wanted to be.

As a child, I wanted to be a singer. I spent every spare moment in my room with my records, singing into a pretend microphone.

∞

I did not care how loud I sang or if anyone noticed. It gave me great joy to sing my heart out. Being a singer was the vision I held for myself. But unfortunately, the world had a different idea for who and what I was to become. The world told me, "That is very cute, Carey, but you are going to college to get a degree so you can have a *real* job." My singing voice stopped—it went completely silent. For many years, there was a flicker of noise, a hint of sound coming from my throat, but it was ultimately drowned out as I focused on climbing that corporate ladder.

Can you relate to this story? Once upon a time, did you possess an authentic, joyful voice that you stopped listening to one day? Was it a conscious decision or did that authentic part of you start to slip away gradually, without you realizing what was happening, until the day came when you realized it was gone?

Most likely, you found that it continued to nag at you. You've probably gone about your job without true joy. To hang in there, you've probably told yourself, "One day I'm going to pursue my dream. One day, when I have more time, more money, and fewer responsibilities, I will go for it."

Many people fill their lives with eating the bottom of the ice cream cone first, thinking they will eventually get to the best part. For most people, by the time they get "there," their ice cream has melted away. Their potential skills have diminished. Maybe they feel too old or have become physically impaired. The opportunity may have passed. They end up living a life of regret.

∞

They come to the end of their life and realize that they never did what God's note instructed, and what they promised to do before they came to earth. This is truly the saddest outcome for any human being.

The good news is that this does not have to be the way anyone's life turns out, most especially yours.

You are about to embark on a journey to bring you back to the authentic person you once were and to help you create your vision. One's vision is everything. With the help of what follows in this book, you will put your vision on paper. You will be invited to describe your vision in as much detail as possible. You will discover what your roadblocks to creating a vision have been and how to set baby-step goals to move you towards your vision.

Before we begin, I encourage you to give yourself the focus you deserve by doing the following four things:

Whether you work through this book in one day or over six weeks, I ask that you commit to unplug from *everything* when you are working with this material. That means no cell phone, no computer, and no other people to distract or influence you. This must be time for just you and your voice. You have probably not listened to your voice exclusively in a while, so prepare to listen to it very closely. Think of the time you spend with yourself and this material as the gift of a retreat you are giving yourself. It is a gift *from you to you*!

∞

1. Record everything you will be asked to write with pen or pencil (maybe even crayon) and paper. No computers. There is a big connection between your hands and your brain, and writing your words out and onto paper embeds the message more deeply within you than typing can ever do. Writing with pen and paper also connects you more deeply to your heart and your authentic being-ness.

2. Do not judge what you write. Keep in mind that many people leave things out because of the embarrassing, yucky stuff they tell themselves. Please take that facet of your identity and lock it in a storage shed as you work with this material. Anyone who has heard me speak knows that my mantra in life is, "No Poopyheads!" Unfortunately, without intending to do so, *we* can be our biggest poopyheads!

3. Another important aspect of this book is that it is a progressive workbook. It is important, therefore, to not skip steps. Please work through this book sequentially and do not move to the next section until the previous one is complete. When you get to the end, you will have a very clear sense of who you are, of what is your vision, and of where you want to go from here.

∞

∞

My promise to you is that what you will create within these pages is only the beginning of your amazing journey. After you write your vision, all sorts of crazy wonderful things will start to happen because you've opened the floodgates. God is standing at those gates waiting for you to let Him in—to guide you to the work He originally assigned to you. All you have to do is stay open and watch as things begin to unfold and connect within your life. This is the beginning of the journey to living your vision. So, together, let's begin ...

How to Use This Book

The chapters of this book are set up so that you can work through them over the course of one solid day, a weekend, or during a dedicated chunk of time once a week for six weeks—completing one of the numbered chapters each week. Based on the current demands of your life, choose which will work best for you.

The key to success is to pick a timeframe and stick with it. If you commit to six weeks, then determine which week you will

∞

begin and plot out six weeks from there. It's optimal if you can go through this book in six consecutive weeks; however, once again, it has to work within your life. If you decide to take one entire day, or a full weekend, carve out that timeframe on your calendar and arrange things in your life so that you can spend the day alone.

Whichever approach you choose, be sure to mark it out on your calendar and commit to the time. Let others know you will be taking time away, even if that place happens to be a room with a closed door within your house. This time is for you and you alone, so set up things in your life to make that possible. For the six-week approach, it will work best to pick the same time each week; however, if that is just not possible, then pick a block of time during each of the six weeks and stick with it.

This book gives you ample space to complete the exercises. However, you may want to do additional journaling, so plan to get a journal, composition notebook, or legal pad in which to write. There is one other feature I want to point out. At the end of every chapter you'll find a box with the words "Infinite Epiphany." This box is intended for you to record any significant insights or aha moments you experience in the chapter. It's those moments that move us or the realizations and ahas we experience that create the biggest changes in our lives. So, be sure to write them down as they occur.

∞

Be gentle with yourself but stay committed. Make a commitment right now that you will stay with this process and see it through to its conclusion. You deserve this gift of time and clarity in order to create the road ahead.

Making a commitment in writing is the best way to stay on track. On the next page is a commitment note for you to sign. As soon as you are ready to start, go ahead and complete it, and let your journey begin.

∞

My Commitment

I, _____, commit to the comple-

tion of this process. I understand that by the end I will have a

clear vision and the action steps to move forward. I have chosen

to complete this book over the course of ___ one day/____ on

weekend/____ six weeks, and have selected the following time-

frames to dedicate to this process:

I will do this work to the best of my ability, staying present to

this process until its completion.

Dated:_____Signed:_____

What is Vision?

*"The only thing worse than being blind
is having sight but no vision."*
- Helen Keller

The Difference Between Dreams and Vision

There is a big difference between having a dream and holding a vision. Most people are dreamers. They constantly talk about "someday." They wait for all of the outside circumstances to change in their lives before they will *be able* to act on their dream. They list issues of time, money, responsibilities, and other outside factors as reasons for not being able to move forward.

I am sorry to report that "someday" will most likely never come. It does not work that way. Having a dream without a vision is kind of like putting the cart before the horse. What most people

∞

do is say things like, "Well, when I don't need this full-time job anymore, I'll start my business," or "When my children are all in school, I'll write my book," or "When I start exercising and lose this extra weight, I'll become a public speaker." We may think that once those outside factors have been addressed, we will begin to step into our dreams, but sadly, we're just fooling ourselves. There will *always* be outside factors—thousands and thousands of them. There is and will always be *something*. For instance, once the kids have begun to attend school, the book may still be just an idea in your head. With their school attendance comes the pull to do volunteer work inside the classroom or on behalf of the school. And once you start exercising and losing weight, more than likely something else will get in the way of jumping on the public speaking circuit. With each factor that seems to get resolved, other factors will appear. It's the nature of life.

We have to acknowledge that outside factors will always be there. There will always be something else, or some other situation, that needs our attention. If we can be honest with ourselves, we will be able to admit that we use those outside factors as excuses to not move forward. So, our dreams stay our dreams, and nothing changes. We live with the status quo.

There is a reason that we use those outside factors to keep us stuck. It's one that most of us have a tough time facing. Plain and simple, we are scared. The truth is that most of us are flat-

∞

out scared to death, and that fear holds us back. It's never about our kids being at home, or the amount of money we have, or our spouse not being as supportive as we wish they would be. It is always about our deepest fears—those fears are what keep us where we are.

Most people's real deep-seated fears are things like fear of failure, fear of success, fear that we can't really do whatever we dream of doing, fear about how we'll do it, and even fears related to whether we deserve our dream or not. So our fears are what hold us back. The moment we can begin to say, "Yes, I have a real fear!" is the moment we can begin to move. Once I can say, "My name is Carey Conley and I am fearful!" I am on my way.

All of the outside factors and excuses are based on what we tell ourselves. Some of what we tell ourselves—those stories and beliefs—go way back. Most likely, they are based on what we were told as children. For instance, although I loved to sing and wanted to become a singer, I was told by *the world* that what I needed to become was someone who worked hard—first in school and then in a job. For years, I believed that if I worked hard and persevered, I would have a satisfying life. The work needed to be demanding in order for me to be successful. Unfortunately, the missing ingredients were passion and authenticity. Without having passion for what I was doing and feeling that my work was an authentic expression of who I was, it was impossible to be and

∞

feel successful.

What we tell ourselves can be based on our fears as well. What we come to believe then becomes our reality. We can create beliefs in our lives based on our past experiences, including traumatic experiences or experiences that devastated us—especially as children. For instance, if we were told that we were a "show off" when we were younger, we may now be afraid to stand up in front of people for fear that they will judge us as being an attention seeker. We have to identify the beliefs we carry, and then decide whether we need to change them. We need to ask ourselves some essential questions:

- What do I tell myself?
- Are those beliefs and stories real?
- Are those beliefs and stories "the truth"?
- Is what I tell myself holding me back?

We have a choice about what we believe. We can continue to believe what we've *always believed*—because those beliefs and stories feel comfortable and our lives feel easier if we stick with them. Or we can step out and make choices about what we will believe and begin to implement changes in our thought processes. At first, it will feel uncomfortable to make these changes. We may feel a bit off balance as we take baby steps towards see-

∞

ing ourselves and our lives in a new way. I guarantee you, though, that the discomfort is worth it.

Beginning to tell ourselves a different story is what makes it possible for us to have a vision. As we connect with our passions, and as we start to see our authentic selves, we are able to begin to create a vision of how we want to show up in the world. I believe that at the moment we create a vision for ourselves, God steps in and says, "I'm going to help you create this." The ripple effect starts. As soon as we claim our vision, especially by writing it down, that ripple effect begins to happen. People and situations present themselves. Opportunities show up. We don't need to wait for outside factors to change, because there will always be something happening in our lives. The situations and events that begin to happen in support of our vision will be bigger than the outside factors we've allowed to hold us back. We simply need to put our stake in the ground and let the magic begin.

∞

Before we go any further, let's take a look at some questions regarding your beliefs and stories. Consider these questions and answer them as truthfully as possible. Write down your answers. Remember that no one else needs to see what you write, unless you choose to share it.

∞

1. What stories and beliefs do you tell yourself? Do they relate to your childhood? Are there people to whom you can attribute those stories and beliefs? Are there past events or circumstances to which you can relate them, even traumatic or devastating moments in your life?

_____

_____

_____

_____

_____

_____

_____

_____

_____

_____

_____

_____

_____

_____

_____

∞

2. Who were you as a child? What were you passionate about? What did you love to do? What did you want to be and/ or do when you grew up? How would you describe the authentic you as a child?

_____

_____

_____

_____

_____

_____

_____

_____

_____

_____

_____

_____

_____

_____

_____

∞

After answering these questions, I'm hopeful that you've come to see how what you've been telling yourself may be preventing you from living the life you envisioned for yourself. I am hopeful that you've also reconnected with the "you" of your childhood—that authentic, vibrant human being who probably saw life as an adventure, not a place full of insurmountable obstacles. Most especially, I am hopeful that you are excited and ready to move into the next parts of this book.

The Benefits of a Clear Vision

Having a vision creates many benefits in a person's life. I believe there are five **key** benefits that result from having a vision. Each of these is a direct result of developing a clear vision and each provides you with big rewards.

#1
You will make better decisions about your money and time, as well as how you invest it and with whom you spend it.

I could write volumes about how the pain of wasted money and time creates stories in people's lives that keep them stuck.

∞

When you know where you are going, you can decide whether to participate in side trips or not. You choose with whom you spend time and money. This is especially important if you are an entrepreneur. The thousands of dollars spent, and time wasted, on buying things and doing activities that don't align with the growth and timing of your business can be astronomical.

A high percentage of business owners quit within the first five years after the start of their business. There are a multitude of reasons to explain why this happens. Two of the reasons I hear frequently from my clients are that they are in debt and they don't have a life. They get massively in debt early on and work way too hard on too many things right up front, rather than identifying specifically what they need to do at each different phase of their business. Plain and simple, they take on way too much too fast.

This often happens because new entrepreneurs step into something they've never done before based on a passion or skill they possess. As a sole entrepreneur, they do it alone, without the help of a coach or adviser, and without delegating any of the responsibilities and duties to anyone else. They have a strong sense that they need to do *everything* so they don't miss *anything*.

New entrepreneurs often look around at what others are doing and decide they need to be doing those same things. Yet

∞

they don't understand that some of what they see others doing is not relevant to them at this early phase in their business's development. They don't understand that someone else may be focusing on a specific set of tasks because they are much further along in the cycle of their business's success. The new entrepreneur bases their actions on what they see others doing rather than on what they and their business truly need.

For instance, in the very beginning, business owners must figure out who they are, what service and/or product they will provide, and what niche they will serve. If they start doing a lot of self-promotion without having these areas identified, individuals can expend and waste a lot of energy, time, and money. In the process of doing all of that, rather than attract clients they repel them. As a result, they begin a cycle of pain. They see that things are not working, so they work harder, throwing more money at their efforts yet not gaining more clients. They do more and spend more, yet they repel people further and further away. In the end, they're exhausted, frustrated, maybe in debt, and they believe there is something wrong with themselves. The comparisons to others deepen.

Debt and exhaustion cause a lot of stress (and oftentimes people keep what is happening to themselves because they feel shame about having accrued debt). So, they begin to isolate because they don't feel like they're being authentic. They're in

∞

their office spiraling down, feeling like a failure, feeling alone, and feeling ashamed. The further down they spiral, the more they isolate. Soon, they have no life outside their work because they have no community with whom they can share what's going on and from whom they can seek counsel. They're working 24/7 to get their business up and running. They think, "I'll just work harder to make the money. That will solve everything." When the money doesn't come or isn't enough to solve their debt, they feel an even bigger sense of failure. The downward cycle continues.

Most of us want to be entrepreneurs to have freedom, yet we often end up working around the clock, desperately trying to get a grasp on our earnings and expenses. We can lose all sense of balance in our lives, and it's not because of choice. Things can get bad enough that our families beg us to quit, which doesn't help us at all. Now, not only do we have our own stress about what is happening in our business, but our families can push at us to quit because nothing is working within the family in terms of time spent together, money coming in, and more. When our families don't see us or the fruits of our labors, they most likely want us to give up and let the business go. And this can lead us to adopt a story about ourselves as a failed entrepreneur who isn't capable of running a business. Yet nothing could be further from the truth!

Having a vision gives you a compass. It helps you decide

∞

whether or not you're staying on track. Your vision is what you look back at each time you consider taking another step or making a change. For instance, if you want a business that you can take with you wherever you go, even if that's working from a vacation condo overlooking the ocean, would expanding to a brick-and-mortar business make sense and be in alignment with that vision?

The best way to make sense of your path is by always looking back at your vision. Reconnecting with your vision helps you funnel your time more efficiently. It helps you look at where to diversify, when to do so, and when to hold where you are at the moment. Using that compass allows you to consider whether something is going to suck your time away from your specific vision. It's important to continually consider where you put your time and focus. In today's world, there are a multitude of activities and opportunities, but not all will benefit you and your business. Not everything out there is going to be helpful. Most will just pull you away from your vision. So always keep your eye on that compass.

∞

#2

Your life becomes much easier and more joyful when you listen to your own truth, your own voice; and that, in turn, makes you more attractive to others. Your excitement and enthusiasm shine and become contagious.

Would you like to have a business where you have more people coming to you versus you having to go out and try to seek them? It's a beautiful place to get to in your business and makes everything more enjoyable.

I do believe that every single one of us was sent to this earth with a very specific mission that we are here to accomplish. As children, we had a sense of it and we were connected to it. Through our upbringing, we lose it. We lose it because it gets "processed" out of us as we grow up and progress through school, even within our social communities.

When people get reattached to their vision and start following it, when they authentically follow what gives them the most joy, what feels most right, when they "lock and load" into their passion, all kinds of things begin to happen. People come into their lives, their confidence grows, they enjoy life more, and they realize how much they love what they're doing. Even if they're

∞

putting a lot of hours into their work, they thrive. Other people start to feel it and feel them—when the person who is living from their vision walks into a networking event, for instance, others will walk across the room to connect with them. It's a whole different energy that we put out when we're doing what we love. Remember, that through everything we do, we either repel or attract others. If we're living our vision and it is based in our authentic purpose, we will continually attract more people and more success.

#3
Your vision becomes the foundation to create the "how."

Don't eat the ice cream cone upside down! Most people wait for the "how" to show up first before they take any action or make any decisions. However, in reality the vision comes first and the "how" shows up as a result of that vision. If you are very structured in your life, you may have a hard time with this concept.

When people believe that the "how" needs to come first, it's like putting the cart before the horse. We wait for outside factors to align, or to go away, or to be resolved. We wait for the "how" to show up—the plan—before we create the vision. When we

∞

take this approach, our vision never gets created. Everything stays status quo.

The vision has to come first in order for the how to begin to fall into place. We need to look at what we want to create in our lives. We look at the specific lifestyle we want to have and we look at the elements we want in our lives. Then we consider all the ways we might create that life and that lifestyle.

Sometimes we need to gather information by talking to people who seem to be doing what might give us the life we want in order to determine what might support that specific life-style. These action steps are still part of the "what." **What** is it that you want to create? **What** might allow you to create that vision? **What** do you want your life to look like? Do you want to work from home, to have a flexible work schedule, to earn a large income, to effect change, to be a leader? **What** might be potential vehicles for bringing that lifestyle to fruition? **What** might support it? Investigate, interview, gather information, and check back with your vision. Does the **"what"** you've gathered fit or support your vision? Only after the vehicles for getting you moving towards your vision are identified can the "how" begin to take shape. Do you need to go to school? Do you need to work in a certain industry, in a certain geographic location, or for a certain company? What training, skills, and experiences do you need to move you towards your vision? Trust the journey. Take the jump and you will build the wings.

∞

#4
Your vision becomes your anchor in the storms of life, which allows you to remain consistent.

Consistency is everything. It helps you remain balanced. Do you ever get derailed from something you start and then lose your focus? This is called "squirrel syndrome." We live in a culture that is overwhelming and filled with a tremendous amount of distractions. When your vision is clear, you can stay the course no matter how big or small the distraction. In life and in business, you can accomplish big feats by taking consistent, bite-size steps every day, no matter what.

There have been multiple setbacks, disappointments, mistakes made, and major shifts in my life, but my vision was always bigger than those walls. I may have taken a day off here and there, but I never quit. Do you want that kind of perseverance? If so, what you need is a GREAT BIG VISION!

When your vision is crystal clear and you want that thing as much as air to breathe, no matter how many obstacles come up—and remember, there are thousands—you have the anchor to keep getting up and climbing over the walls. None of what you do and none of what happens matters if you can't get up and get over the walls—those obstacles are bound to happen.

∞

For example, in the beginning of most businesses people receive a lot of rejection. The very people you may think will be your biggest cheerleaders may turn out not to be. Especially because they love you and want to protect you, they may think your idea is crazy and they may believe that what you're trying to accomplish is impossible. Remember, they want to keep you safe, and they don't have your vision.

You have to understand that your vision is *your vision.* What you see is what you see. Don't expect others to see it the way you do. Don't expect them to even see it at all. They can't because they have their own vision, their own perspective. And because they can't see your vision, they want to protect you from failure.

You may start to experience self-doubt. You may experience rejection. The walls may get bigger. You may be moving towards success, and actually seeing it, and then something happens—that can be another wall. For instance, maybe you've been spreading your wings as a leader and then you make some mistakes. Quite possibly, those mistakes cause you to crash and burn, or they may cause a big setback in your forward momentum. When and if that happens, it is easy to want to bail—to retreat and want to give up. At that moment, however, you need to do the exact opposite. Maybe you need to take a break and lick your wounds. But then you need to return to your vision and remember why you wanted what you wanted. Remember your vision of having relief from

財financial stresses, of having the ability to travel, and of creating a flexible work schedule. Once you return to that vision, it can override any tragedy, any traumatic event, and any wall. Your vision once more becomes the thing you want more than any bad thing that happens. In order for that to happen, though, your vision has to be *big enough* and you have to want it *bad enough*. Then, no matter what happens in your life, your vision will keep you going.

#5
Vision is leadership and allows you to change not only your world but impact the world of others around you: your children, your family, your community, your co-workers.

If you want to make a difference, be a leader with a strong purpose and path. Nobody follows a wishy-washy leader. How often do presidential hopefuls try to cast their opponents as "wishy-washy"? If your vision is diluted, step into it and become the leader you are meant to be.

Vision is so important because it *is* leadership. In anything we step into, we have to make a choice first to lead ourselves before we will be able to lead others. And we cannot be a strong leader without a strong vision. People get scared because they think

∞

they have to have it all figured out and be perfect from the very start. Then, they don't step into a leadership role because they don't have things figured out. We desperately want and need to be leaders in our own lives. In order to do that, we have to go against the grain of what everyone else does—being followers and believing that they're entitled to have things come to them.

You have to create a vision first in order to become a leader who affects change. You have to have the vision first, a strong enough one that people can then see themselves becoming a part of it—that's what makes a great leader. Your vision needs to be big enough that it makes people want to join you. However, you have to be willing to lead yourself first so that others will follow you. People will then want to attach to what you're doing and become a part of your vision.

A big vision that draws people to you is one that requires you to step out of the box and be willing to become something bigger than having only a personal vision. It becomes about leaving a legacy—about creating something that will make an impact in the world. A vision such as that is big enough to sweep up others into the wave of its movement.

If your vision is exclusively personal, if it is murky, it will be more difficult to stay the course. If your vision is all about you—if it is *only* about you—it becomes easier to walk away when the going gets rough. If you have a tendency to quit your vision,

∞

it's probably because you're making it all about you. When you attach your vision to other people and to the knowledge that others are counting on you, then it's harder to walk away from your vision. It's also harder for the other people to walk away from you and your vision. The bigger the vision, the more people with be drawn to you and to what you want to create.

The bottom line is that creating and maintaining a vision is a choice that brings a whole lot of "awesome" into your life. The key word here is "choice." It means choosing faith over fear. The fear never goes away in order for you to begin. If everything were perfectly orchestrated, then why would you need faith? Every single person who has ever stepped into their greatness and achieved success did it with one common trait: they chose faith and they chose to listen to one voice only—their own.

Vision takes a leap of faith, because you're going to be met with all sorts of adversity and pushback. You have to take a leap of faith first. Fear and faith cannot exist in the same time and space. It's a non-negotiable. So minute by minute, you are acting out of fear or you are acting out of faith. Most people act out of fear.

Most people also think that successful people have no fear. Successful people will tell you that the bottom line is that every-one has fear, but even while acknowledging that fear is there, they step out in faith. Their actions are based in faith even though fear is present. That takes courage.

∞

The key to successful people is that they have fear but choose not to act on it. They learn to have a different relationship with fear. They put it in its place and then act on faith. They don't make decisions or take actions based in fear. They identify the fear and where it's coming from, then they acknowledge it and proceed. They put the fear in its place. They don't deny it or try to push it away—they acknowledge it and move forward in faith and belief. This is true courage!

There's always a choice to step out in faith and trust in the belief that the plan will be revealed as you proceed. A little bit of faith goes a long way! So feel the fear and do it anyway.

Infinite Epiphany

Everything Starts with You

"Man stands in his own shadow and wonders why it's dark."
- Zen Proverb

If we take a leap of faith and create a vision—and if that vision is bigger than we are—when difficult events and circumstances occur in our lives our vision will be sustainable. Through difficult times, that vision can even sustain us. When adversity happens or we experience pushback in our lives, our vision can override that adversity. When our vision is bigger than we are, it will be bigger than any adversity we face.

For instance, after my husband died tragically, I could have walked away from my work and my vision. In fact, many of those closest to me suggested I take at least a year away from my work to come to terms with my loss. They expressed that they knew I was in shock and they pointed out that I did not need to work for

∞

financial reasons. There was truth in their concerns and observations; however, my vision has always been bigger than me and my life. And knowing who I truly am, I saw that my work would actually help me in my healing process. I am wired to work—it is therapy for me, especially because I am usually surrounded by positive people. For me, having the opportunity to stay plugged into my work and to serve others was and continues to be extremely therapeutic and a source of positive energy in my life.

Your vision statement has to be huge; it needs to be something bigger than you. When you create such a vision, it goes beyond your basic needs and your own life. A big vision reaches beyond your immediate world. When your vision is bigger than you, it is so big that no matter what happens in your life it can propel you to keep moving forward.

In order to get to such a vision, though, we need to first look at a few basic truths. There are three truths I've come to understand that relate directly to each person's ability to take a leap of faith and create a big vision. These truths have everything to do with our perceptions about our lives and about life in general. We can choose to see our lives as happening to us, where things occur and we have no control over what takes place, including how we respond to events and circumstances. Or we can see our lives as opportunities to grow, evolve, and to serve others. Events may happen over which we have little or no control, but those

∞

who see life as the chance to grow understand that what we do in response to circumstances and events can make the difference between being a victim and being responsible for one's own life.

Let's take a look at each of these three fundamental truths.

Truth #1: Everyone holds a core truth that impacts and influences the way we view our lives and how we live it. This deep-seated truth is either negative, neutral, or positive.

Based on one of these three foundational perspectives, we make choices throughout our lives.

> **Negative truth =** These people see their lives as only getting worse. Most likely, this is not you, since you have picked up this book and have begun to work with it. But do you know anyone who always talks about how bad things are, whether they are talking about their job, their relationships, schools, churches, and/or the government? Their perspective is one of total doom and gloom.

> **Neutral truth =** These individuals do not see that much will ever change and they are willing to be

∞

content with maintaining that perspective. Sadly, this describes most of the population.

Positive truth = These individuals see great things coming in the future. That perspective drives them to keep moving towards the future.

∞

Your Turn: Ask yourself, honestly, which core truth do you hold?

_____

_____

_____

_____

Here's a clue. Start to monitor what you hear yourself say. What comes out of your mouth on a regular basis? If you are bold enough to pick one safe person in your life, have them repeat what they hear you say and even the tone you use when you make statements. Often we are unaware that with the words we choose and the way we speak, we are actually breathing life into our circumstances and our life perspective.

∞

Truth #2: The universe does not care what your vision is, but it does respond to it, and *that* vision is the one that gets created.

Do you wonder why your life evolves the way it does? Truth: YOU and your thoughts create it. The good news! YOU can attract a whole new life simply by choosing it. Isn't that exciting?

I would never want you to belittle any of your life's circumstances or to judge your life harshly. After all, every single one of us has had our share of major blows. What we don't want to do, though, is to define ourselves by our negative experiences. Once we stop defining ourselves and our lives by those experiences, we will *stop attracting them.*

Whatever your current circumstances may be, it's essential that you accept where you are at this moment in time. You must acknowledge the truth of what is and where you are, which is very different from defining yourself by what is and has been happening. From this place of acknowledging the truth, you can go to work on changing your thoughts and the stories you tell yourself—the stories you currently believe as real. This is not an easy overnight process. It is a journey.

Are you willing and prepared to take 100% responsibility for how your life looks now and stop breathing life into the circumstances you no longer want by eliminating those past experiences from your thoughts and words? Are you willing to begin

∞

the journey from how things look now to what they can become?

Let's take two minutes right now for you to write down what you hear yourself say about your life. I ask that you be completely truthful here and that you not judge anything you write. It's important that you remain as neutral as possible as you write, because any emotion that you bring into this can cause you to judge what you're writing. This exercise is meant for observation only, so please do not leave anything out. It's also essential that you look at what you've written as unemotionally and as objectively as possible. Judging what you write defeats the purpose.

_____

_____

_____

_____

_____

_____

_____

_____

_____

_____

_____

∞

Now take a look at what you've written. Do you recognize a pattern or patterns? If so, list them here.

_____

_____

_____

_____

_____

_____

_____

Truth #3: Your motivation is directly sourced in your vision. Your vision will either propel you to move forward or to be stuck.

Do you find that you can't seem to get yourself moving towards what you say you want to do? Does that awareness make you uncomfortable in some way? Do you have a clear sense of why that may be?

Quite simply, my belief is that your vision is not clear enough or big enough to propel you forward. You have not yet identified it or it is not yet compelling enough to sustain you. Your vision must also be authentic.

∞

An authentic vision is one that means so much to the individual that they'll eventually be propelled forward, with or without any outside help. When we are crystal clear about what we want to create, nothing can or will derail us and our forward momentum.

As a coach, when I work with individuals, I do not expect to motivate them. My role and responsibility is to inspire, mentor, and teach my clients how to listen to their authentic voice, how to get to their vision, and how to attach to it. Their motivation, however, has to come from within themselves. I give them the template to use, a roadmap to follow, and the space and the time to create their vision, but the vision has to come from them.

It is like exercising. I honestly do not like to exercise. I seem to avoid it at all costs. I can hire someone to give me an exercise program to follow, I can pay thousands of dollars to have a customized regimen created, and even the equipment or facility to use, but if I am not motivated to exercise I will find a way out of it. The bottom line is that if I don't want this for myself, I won't do it. If my motivation is not sourced directly back to my desire to do this for myself, the exercise program will not be successful.

∞

Stories

Frankly, there are some very common themes that trip people and keep them from creating a clear vision. People, in general, blame the outside circumstances in their lives for preventing them from going after their visions. Take a look at the list below and see if you recognize any of these:

- I don't have the money.
- I don't have the time.
- I don't have the education.
- I don't have the support.
- I don't know how.
- I need to get some things off my plate first.
- I need to be thinner/smarter/better looking ...

These are all examples of the stories we tell ourselves. These represent the excuses we come up with that prevent us from creating a big vision and from moving forward. These excuses come as a result of the "comfort zone" life we create to justify to ourselves and the world why we can't go after our vision right now.

I choose the word "stories" intentionally to make a bigger point. These are the things we talk about. We believe them and we act *from them, because of them*, or *in support of them*. These

∞

are not the truth—they are the reality we create based on what we tell ourselves.

Someday

People live in *someday* mentality. Guess what? *Someday* does not exist on the calendar. You can play that game all you want, but you are going to die with that word in your vocabulary, and nothing else, unless you are brave enough to embrace the hardest truth of all: it starts with YOU and it starts NOW.

Reading my last statement that everything starts with YOU and it all starts NOW may be causing you a bit of discomfort. You may even be squirming in your chair or thinking about putting this book down for a while—maybe even *forever.* I urge you not to stop. I promise that if you hang in here you're going to be so grateful that you did. At this very moment, you are *very close* to creating your vision.

Chances are that in the past you've lived in *someday* mentality. Maybe you're living in it right now. So, before we move on, let's take a brief look at what has been getting in your way up to now. Remember that this is for your eyes only. You don't need to share this with anyone, so please be as honest as you can.

∞

1. Take a moment to identify what you think your roadblocks really are. What are your deepest fears? List them.

----

2. Take some time now to uncover and record what the "real things" are that you've been claiming as the reasons for not moving forward in your life. List them, being completely honest and withholding all judgment, blame, or shame. Again, these are the circumstances and situations that look a certain way right now (e.g., "I don't have enough money to pay my bills, so I cannot start my business yet"). They may be the "things" that are keep-

∞

ing you from moving forward but, believe me, they are not actually the reason you don't move forward.

Let me give you an example. I recently worked with a client and asked her, "So, tell me something that you've been telling yourself about why you aren't moving forward in your business." She replied, "I cannot yet purchase the equipment I need. I can't acquire it because I don't have the money to pay for it." I then asked her if she knew of other people who'd gotten the money they needed to move forward and she answered that she did. "So," I said, "can we agree that it's not really the money?" When she replied, "Yes," I asked her what she thought the real reason was. She responded, "I don't believe I can really do it. I'm scared." We have to peel back the layers of the onion to get to our deeper issues.

_____

_____

_____

_____

_____

_____

_____

_____

∞

_____

_____

_____

_____

_____

_____

_____

∞

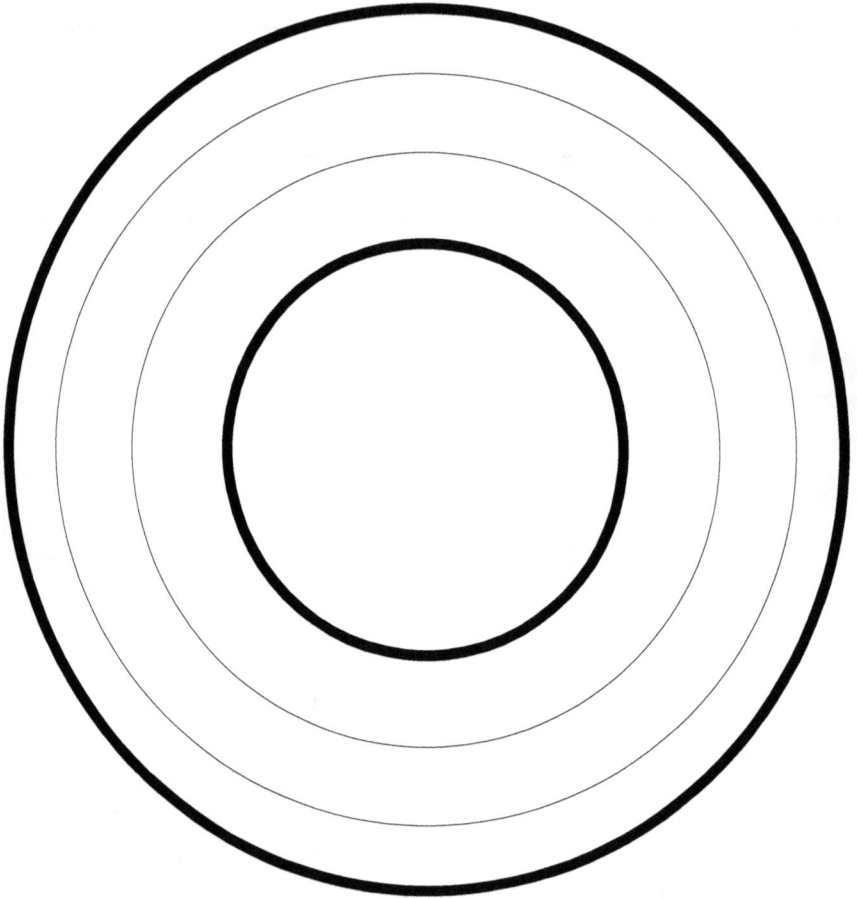

∞

Target Exercise

Let's pause here to complete one of my favorite exercises. I love it because it can open one's eyes to the difference between what they believe is happening and what is actually occurring. I call it the "Target Exercise," and it reveals to us how we may believe the ripple effect works, yet what actually happens.

To begin, use the outer section of the target on the opposite page to write all the justifications you currently use that stop you from creating your vision. Take two minutes to do that.

Next, write "ME" in the bullseye. Be sure to write it as big as you possibly can.

Now consider the following questions. They will help you gain a better understanding of your personal truth and where you've been up to now:

- Are you one of those individuals who waits for outside circumstances to change before you can begin to focus on ME, on the center of the target?

- Do you expect "dreams" and all the right circumstances and events to ripple from the outside in before you can begin to think about creating the life you want to live?

∞

People usually wait for their outer circumstances to change before they will begin to go after their dreams. Most people live as if the ripple will come to them. They wait, but unfortunately ripples don't work that way. It's like trying to eat the ice cream cone from the bottom up—this creates a very chaotic, unfulfilled, and messy life.

So let's turn this around. In actuality, a ripple goes outward. It's up to us to create the ripple from within ourselves and send it out. What has to happen is the ME (the center of the target) must go to work to create what you want. When you do, it won't matter what those outer circumstances are.

And that's exactly what happens when we create a big vision— it's us working from the inside out. Having a big enough vision will take care of many of the popular, almost award-winning, excuses universally claimed as reasons to stay in a neutral zone. When you accept that your vision starts with "ME," without the "yeah, buts," the vision of your life ripples outward. Crazy, amazing, wonderful results happen, line up, and assist you to get you moving in the direction of where you want to go.

You have the power to start creating the ripple in your life right now. That power has been there all along. Yes, it's important to acknowledge all those outside circumstances you deal with—because they aren't going to go away—but the good news is that you don't have to give them as much power as you've

∞

given them in the past. The bigger you can write your ME, the bigger you create your vision, the more powerful the ripple effect will be.

3. Are you willing to accept that you are 100% responsible for everything that's happened in your life up to now? If so, acknowledge that you are responsible for everything you've created in your life. Write this as a statement to yourself. Acknowledgment is the catalyst for change!

_____

_____

_____

_____

_____

_____

_____

_____

Every single one of us was sent here to fulfill something that no one else can do. There is no mistake as to how each of us is wired. We each have a purpose for being here. You were sent here with a mission. You have a purpose for being here, and it is unique to you. When you tap into your purpose, you feel passionate about it. When you are doing what you were meant to do, you cannot walk away from it. You cannot quit your purpose. If you try to quit, you'll find yourself feeling unhappy, most likely losing hope and feeling that life is meaningless.

Creating your authentic vision allows you to tap into your reason for being here. And once you tap into it, you are given everything you need to fulfill your mission. God stands at the gate waiting for you to open it. Your treasures, hopes, and dreams are wrapped in one little box that He holds for you. Invite the process to begin.

It is time to move into your purpose. It is time to declare your readiness to proceed. Are you ready to get to work on your authentic vision and to get started creating it? Are you ready to make a commitment to yourself, to make a dedication to yourself that will then lead to the creation of your vision? Are you ready to be a leader, to have a vision, and to take baby steps towards that vision?

If you've answered "yes" to each of these questions, then turn the page and let's start *visioning*!

Infinite Epiphany

3

Your Three-Year Vision

"The best way to predict the future is to create it."
- Abraham Lincoln

This chapter is my *favorite* part of the process! I never get tired of working with people to create their three-year vision because I know the power it holds. What others have experienced and shared with me as a result of this process makes the hair on my arms stand up. When people go through this series of exercises as part of my workshops, I see their transformations happen right before my eyes. I witness them as they make major breakthroughs in what has been keeping them stuck and what they really want in their lives. The direction they want to go becomes so clear and they are so willing to make it unfold that what happens next, often within days of leaving the workshop, seems like a miracle. I love the phone calls I receive that start out, "You're not going to believe what happened to me today!"

When I went through this process for the first time in 1988, I was completely lined up with listening to God and feeling how right, authentic, and true my three-year vision was. I felt it down to my soul. And because I "locked and loaded" into that vision as soon as I'd written it, the ripple effect started almost immediately. All sorts of things began to take place, and each time they did I knew they were a part of what I had written. My three-year visions have served me well for many, many years. They still do. Whenever an "opportunity" presents itself, I know whether to act on it or not. I am able to determine whether something is a part of my vision or doesn't line up and then can respond accordingly.

In addition to creating a three-year vision, I also have five- and ten-year vision statements. For most people, however, visioning three years into the future is far enough to go. Especially because we live in a world where most people don't even think about where they are going to be in three months, to envision and ask beyond three years can be a huge challenge. In our current way of living, the majority of us could be termed as the "right-now" society. So, I'm not going to ask you to go beyond three years in this exercise. *Whew!*

∞

∞

Before we go any further, I need you to place yourself in a quiet place where you will be able to have a period of uninterrupted time. If you are reading this chapter and are not in a quiet space, then don't attempt this process yet and don't move ahead in the book. Trust me on this. This is essential.

If you cannot complete this process right now, please consider where you'll need to go to do it. Is there a space or room that will provide you with a quiet environment and uninterrupted time? If one is not readily available to you, can you identify somewhere that can provide you with the time and space you'll need? Once you identify the place, schedule a time on your calendar as soon as possible to retreat to it. If you're already in that space, then let's move forward!

Part One: The Three-Year Exercise

Allow *at least* an hour to complete the three-part self-discovery that begins here. Take yourself to that comfortable place you've previously identified. We will start with the non-negotiables of life. The non-negotiables refer to time; the fact that life, circumstances, and our lifestyles change as time passes; and the

∞

process of aging—your aging and your family's, including your children and parents.

Now grab your pen or pencil. At the top of page 57, put the date that represents three years from today.

On the next three lines, write down the following numbers in relation to three years from today, as if it is that date now:

1. Your age;
2. The ages of your children, if you have them, or other children in your life who you are close to; and
3. The ages of your parents, if they are still alive and you are involved in their lives.

Why would I have you start with these? Because, unlike the things we talked about in the last chapter that are *in* your control, these are the things that are *not*. God willing, three years from now, you will be older and so will your loved ones.

Most people live in complete denial about the fact that everyone will age. They try and negotiate with time. They think they have all the time in the world. They go through each day as if they have more than twenty-four hours. The reality is that we cannot change the number of hours in a day or a week, a month or a year, and we cannot stop anyone, including ourselves, from aging.

Most people also think that looking ahead to three years from now is too far into the future to think about. They believe they

∞

have plenty of time to prepare for what their lives will look like at any future date. Unfortunately, in almost the blink of an eye, three years will pass and those same people will wonder where the time has gone. They look back and are shocked as they realize they can never get the past back.

I distinctly remember standing at my son's high school graduation, thinking: *What just happened? One day he was two, standing beside me as a little boy, and the next, he is walking down that aisle as a young man preparing to leave for college.* BAM! Our life as a family was about to shift.

If you have kids in your life, you probably have experienced these happy/sad moments. But here's the difference. Years ago, before my son was born, I wrote a vision statement. I chose to get off the corporate track and begin my first business at home to create the life and relationship with my son and his sister that I intended to sustain us for a lifetime. As a result, I was filled with a lot of emotion at his graduation but, I'm happy to say, not one of those feelings was regret.

The issues most people struggle with at the moment of their child's graduation were much easier because I had prepared. As I watched him graduate, I had no regrets that I hadn't financially prepared for his college years ahead or emotionally prepared for the day he would be leaving home. I had no regrets about not having spent enough time with him, because I had envisioned

∞

and shaped my life to work at home, knowing how precious my time would be with my children. For the most part, I'd kept my work life and family life balanced. More importantly, as prepared as I felt for this monumental moment in our lives, my son was prepared, too.

Later in this chapter, you'll be writing your own vision letter. When you do, you may be able to see how different your life might look at a milestone age or what might be happening with your parents as they age. Saying "we will cross that bridge when we get there" does not pay the college tuition nor give you the financial stability to take time off to support your family— whether that's aging parents or young children. Denial is *wishy-washy* living. And *wishy-washy* living produces a wishy-washy life!

Part Two: The Three-Minute Scoop

In a few moments, you're going to take three minutes to write everything you see your life looking like as if it were three years from now. Below are listed the 5 Fs of life: faith/community, family/friends, fitness/health, finance/career, and foundations. Within each of these categories are a series of questions that are meant to serve as prompts as you consider these key components of your life. Keeping in mind the date you wrote that

∞

represents three years from today, I want you to read through each of the groups of questions to mentally consider how your life will look then.

1. *Faith/Community:*
   - Is serving important to you? If so, what does that look like?
   - Are you involved in your church/the school/the neighborhood?
   - What specific role do you play?

2. *Family/Friends* (those you "allow" close to you and spend time with):
   - Where do you live? In what city or town? In which neighborhood? What does your living situation look like? Do you live in an apartment? A house? Is it large or small? Do you have a yard or garden? Do you live in a high-rise? In the mountains? In an urban, rural, or suburban setting?
   - What does your family look like? How do you spend time together?
   - Who else do you spend time with? What do you do together? Where do you go?

∞

- What do you do for entertainment? For work and/or play?

3. *Fitness/Health:*

- How do you look and feel?
- What do you enjoy doing to stay fit?
- Is staying fit and healthy important to you?

4. *Finance/Career:*

- How will you finance the lifestyle you envision three years from now?
- Describe your employment or source of income.
- How is your business structured to support you?
- How much is the business making?
- How big is your bank account/business revenue?

5. *Foundation:*

- What behavioral characteristics have you developed?
- How do you want to be remembered?
- What would you like people to say about you as a person?

∞

With these questions in mind and the answers you see in your head, you are now going to write for the next three minutes. The ice cream scoop on the following page is where you will list everything that comes to mind based on the questions you just considered. There is no need to go back to the list of questions. Simply write down everything that comes to mind during the three minutes and be sure to not leave anything out—no matter what you have or have not done in the past, or because you fear failure or success, or you do not see the "how." "How" comes after the vision, remember?

Now you're ready to begin. Set your timer for three minutes, turn the page, and start writing inside your scoop ... GO!

∞

Date: _____

_____ _____ _____

∞

At the end of three minutes, it's time to write down what "epiphanies" you had about what you wrote:

How do you feel about what you've written?

_____

_____

_____

_____

_____

_____

_____

What things on your list scare you? Why? What fears do they bring up as you look at them?

_____

_____

_____

_____

_____

_____

∞

_____

_____

What items on your list excite you? Why?

_____

_____

_____

_____

_____

_____

_____

What items on your list will take major changes in your life as it is right now to create in the future?

_____

_____

_____

_____

_____

_____

∞

Part Three: The Three-Year Letter

Now we're going to dive deeper and put a stake in the ground. Get cozy because you are going to give this vision flavor. For the "how" to evolve, your vision cannot be a "hope, a wish, and a prayer." You have to articulate it so clearly that when you share it with others, they can see it, taste it, touch it, and smell it. It takes on a life of its own—it becomes a living, breathing entity.

As you begin, pretend you are writing a letter to someone you have not spoken to in three years. You intend to catch up with them on your life—all the things that have happened during the past three years, as well as what you are doing now and where you are headed. You can write this letter to anyone you choose, including me. I love reading the three-year letters, so I invite you to send this to me via my email (carey@careyconley.com). I promise to treasure it and respond to you with a gift.

I encourage you to write this letter to someone you consider safe. The very person you may *want* to share this with in the hope that they will get excited for and with you may be the very person who will be afraid of your vision. They may then attempt to diminish or counter your vision and your joy. Do not expect other people to see what you see. When you learn this life lesson, it will save you energy and heartache. These people love you and, because they can't see what you see, they may want to pro-

∞

tect you from something they are afraid will hurt you. I learned a long time ago to choose very carefully who I share my plans and goals with and not to judge the ones who don't or can't get it.

Here are rules for writing your letter:

1. Write the letter with the person in mind who you plan to have read it.

2. Allow sufficient time to write your letter. You'll need at least an hour, but you may find you need a whole day.

3. Most people downplay their lives. This is your opportunity to go for your favorite ice cream flavor. Nothing is too grandiose. Do not leave anything out because of the past or the messages in your head that tell you all the reasons you *can't*. Doubt and fear kill—visions, dreams, and any forward motion.

4. Avoid words like "hoping, trying, wanting, etc." These are wishy-washy words. Words have power. Use strong, affirmative words like, "I *have*, I *did*, I *am* ..."

5. Give your letter a lot of detail. Remember the questions you considered earlier in this chapter and the ice cream scoop you filled with your vision? Describe them here, bringing in as many of the senses as you can so that you and your reader can experience your vision to its fullest. Bring your vision into full, living color so that whoever

∞

reads it will be able to see it in all its brilliance with their mind.

For instance, in your three-year vision, do you have a house? Is it on a mountaintop, in a swanky suburb, or in the middle of a busy urban city? Why do you love it? What do you enjoy doing there? Do you see yourself going on trips? If so, where? Are you sailing around the Bahamas, climbing Mt. Everest, visiting Washington, D. C.? Are you flying, driving, or riding a horse—maybe even a camel? Who is with you? Get the picture? This is where you're going to describe everything you see in your life as they relate to the 5 Fs of life: faith/community, family/friends, fitness/health, finance/career, and foundations.

Remember the target we worked with in the last chapter? What you are about to create is your bullseye. This is your ME! This is your vision that begins the ripple effect in your life. Once you write this, God and the universe will align with you and what you've written to bring it into focus.

So get ready ... eliminate all distraction, including phones and computers ... set your timer for at least an hour ... GO!

∞

∞

∞

∞

∞

∞

∞

∞

∞

_____

_____

_____

_____

_____

_____

_____

_____

_____

_____

_____

_____

_____

_____

_____

_____

_____

_____

_____

∞

It Is Powerful!

Congratulations! Your three-year vision letter is written! Hope is renewed! People get excited about their lives again, and I imagine that is already beginning to happen for you. Most importantly, you can now begin to work on breaking down what you've written into bite-size pieces for the ultimate creation ... the life God intended you to live.

As I stated before you wrote your letter, I encourage you to share this *only* with people who are safe. The person or people you choose are the ones who will get excited along with you. They might even ask how they can help or offer to assist with something you shared.

Remember, that ripple effect? Well, it has already begun! How fast your vision manifests depends on what you do next. For right now, though, before we go any further, do something to reward yourself for doing the one thing that fewer than three percent of the population accomplishes: You've just given your vision a form. Most especially, you've given it a voice.

Infinite Epiphany

4

Obstacles

"Rule of Thumb: The more important a call or action is to our soul's evolution, the Resistance we will feel towards pursuing it."
- Steven Pressfield

Have you ever thought of and planned a goal? Have you written and rewritten that goal and before you knew it, years passed without your goal having been accomplished? Sadly, this is the case for most people. The majority of us write goals that remain dormant and never actually get completed.

In Chapter 5, you will put down your goals *again* in writing. This time, however, you have the chance to really accomplish them. In this chapter, you will complete an exercise that will help you unlock the mystery to identify the "stories" that generate obstacles to your goals.

When you wrote your three-year vision letter in Chapter 3, there were probably voices in your head saying things like, "You

∞

aren't smart enough"; "You tried that and failed before, so what makes you think you can do it now?"; "Other people have more talent than you"; "You aren't worthy or deserving of such a 'charmed' life." These are just a few of the many, many messages that play in our heads before, during, and after we take *any* steps to make changes in our lives. And these become the source of our biggest obstacles.

The last statement is most prevalent for women. How does anyone even begin to believe themselves unworthy? If you are interested in pursuing the science and deeper answers to this question, there are many amazing books available on neuropathy that go into detail about how those messages plant themselves and grow. However, for the sake of focus and moving forward, realize that those messages came in through one of two ways and are now part of your "story."

The first way you build a story is from things you were told by your tribe—those loving, well-meaning people who either raised you or educated you on what to expect from the world. They passed down values because someone gave those tenets to *them*, and without really thinking whether or not they held true, those beliefs were handed down to the next generation.

Can you identify anything you hear yourself say that could be a tribal message? Do you recognize family characteristics that may sound something like: "That may work for other people

∞

but not for us"; "Our family has never been good at ..."; "People with money are usually mean, egotistical, or selfish"; "We don't dream; we work hard"; or "You have Uncle Chester's big bones ..."? Consider jealousy and manipulated thinking that you might have picked up from others, which can be reflected in questions such as, "Why would you want to risk doing something like *that*?"

Write down as many of those thoughts and beliefs about yourself as you can think of right now. Remember, these are the thoughts and beliefs that have come from your family, friends, and institutions rather than from you:

_____

_____

_____

_____

_____

_____

_____

_____

_____

_____

_____

∞

_____

_____

_____

_____

_____

_____

_____

_____

In the words of Dr. Phil, "How's that workin' for ya?" Are those individuals who sound more like critics than cheerleaders achieving their dreams or living in "someday" with regret and very little joy?

One of my strongest mentors, Rita Davenport, said, "Do not take advice from people more messed up than you." This may sound harsh, but we tend to embrace their messages and hold them as our truths. As a result, they become our stories. When they do, we hear ourselves saying things like, "I can't build my own business because no one in my family has ever been an entrepreneur."

The second way you develop stories stems from emotional events that have occurred in your life. The past event creates

∞

such an impact that you use it to perpetuate a reality that holds you back in the present.

For instance, when I was building my Arbonne business, selling health and beauty products, I hovered at the level below the anticipated accomplishment of a vice president for over four years. Others came in and were elevated to that level much faster than I. It was frustrating and demoralizing. I finally realized I was stuck in a story where I told myself the other women had some secret activity they were not sharing with me. I truly believed they would see me at meetings, smile at me, and tell me how awesome I was, but then they would meet somewhere in private to discuss what they were *really* doing to succeed. The saddest part of this story is that it had its foundation in an event that happened to me in *middle school.*

It may be hard to understand the powerful impact that the past event had on my work situation at the time, but I totally believed it. The moment I realized where this story came from, and that it was *not* truth, everything changed! Once I was able to see the old story and acknowledge how it was keeping me from moving forward, I was able to rewrite a new story. And as a result, I ultimately attained vice president level.

Think of any event or events that may have created a story and are now affecting, or have the potential to affect, your life currently. Write them down below.

∞

∞

To get a taste of how you can poke and prod these "old stories" that hold you back in your life, let's take some time now to do a two-part eye-opening activity. For this activity I ask that you get a notebook containing paper you can tear out or a couple sheets of loose paper. When you are finished with this exercise, you'll want to do a ceremony or ritual with the paper. The exercise is printed here in the book, but I recommend that you use separate paper so you'll be able to release it when you're done.

On the first of the two pieces of paper create two columns by drawing a line down the center. Label the left-hand column, "What did you hear yourself saying when you wrote your letter?" Label the right-hand column with the question, "Where did it come from?" Take a moment here to think about what happened when you wrote your three-year vision letter. What did you hear yourself saying to yourself as you wrote your letter? What statements did you say to yourself that made you pause or even consider not finishing the letter? What thoughts came through that made you doubt what you were writing? What sentiments did you hear yourself expressing that challenged you to not write any part of your vision down on paper? Write down everything you heard without any judgment or emotion. The purpose of recording these thoughts is for you to see what may be at the root of why you find yourself not able to move forward.

Now, on the right-hand side of the page, record where these

∞

ideas and beliefs came from. Remember that they were either learned through others or created as a result of event(s). As with the left-hand column, do not judge any of what you write down. Blaming others or beating yourself up will only create more emotion, and any emotion wrapped around this exercise will prevent you from being able to see clearly "what is and has been." Observe everything you write without layering any emotion on top of it. Emotion will keep you from truly understanding, so this is a time to be as neutral as possible. The purpose of what you are writing on this page and the next one is to uncover and observe. We cannot change what we are not aware of. We cannot change what we don't know. So, be an observer and allow yourself to learn more about what has been creating obstacles in your life up to this point.

On the second piece of paper, you're again going to create two columns. Label the left-hand column "Old Story" and the right-hand column "New Story." In the left-hand column write down the "stories" you listed earlier. If you're not certain what those old stories might be, think about what you hear yourself say repeatedly to explain why you're not going after your vision or not able to pursue it. As you write them down, again think about where they originated. Was it via a message you received in your life or as a result of an event that happened?

After you've recorded as many "old stories" as you can recall,

∞

go back and read each one individually. For each one, tell your-self that you can now admit this is just a story and not the truth.

Next, on the right-hand column, for each old story create a new story. This is your opportunity to rewrite what you say to yourself. The new stories can be written as affirmations, start-ing the sentences with phrases such as "I am," "I have," "I will," "I've done," "I'm doing," etc. Notice the power in statements that begin with phrases such as these. They are affirmative and action-oriented. They also denote the way things are now—for you and your life—which is the catalyst for them becoming your reality.

When I realized the old story that was preventing me from moving into a vice president position with Arbonne, I wrote a new story. Before I actually became a vice president, I made statements such as, "I am a national vice president in Arbonne," and "I have always been a national vice president in Arbonne."

This is your chance to rewrite what you're saying to yourself, so that you too can begin to live your vision.

To anchor in this exercise even deeper, take the second piece of paper and rip it down the middle along the line you made. Take the "old story" portion of the page and create a ritual, cer-emony, or celebration with friends around its release. Have fun with this. The goal is to release these old stories, so you can burn the piece of paper or bury it—anything that allows you to really

∞

let the old stories go. You might come up with words to speak as you burn the paper or bury it in the ground. You might choose to tear the half-sheet into small pieces before you burn or bury them. Do whatever feels comfortable and clearly sends the message that you are releasing these old stories *forever*.

Now take the half-sheet containing the new stories and hang them or place them where you can see them regularly. You can rewrite these affirmations or statements and place copies in prominent places, such as on your bathroom mirror, your computer, in your office, and in your kitchen—anywhere and everywhere you'll be able to see them and reread them again and again. Use your affirmations as a new tool to deepen your new truth and change what you say to and about yourself. Remember that any affirmations you write need to begin with words such as "I am, I have, I've done, I'm doing..." Some people record their affirmations in their own voice so they can listen to them over and over. Hearing your own voice state your affirmations is an extremely powerful way to take in your new beliefs. What you see and hear anchors in your vision and programs your new story.

I recently read *The War of Art* by Steven Pressfield. In his book, he speaks about what holds us back from our purpose. He states that fear is not God-driven. It comes from the *one force* that tries to keep you from the *one thing* you're born to do. The more you come closer to following your inner voice and pursuing

∞

your vision, the bigger the walls and obstacles will become that try to prevent you from living your vision. The irony is that the bigger the walls and obstacles confronting you, the bigger and closer you are to something really big. It's important for each of us to identify what that "something big" is and go for it.

It's also important to identify what the real resistance is. Remember, it's never the outside stuff. The only person stopping you is you. The resistance comes from something you learned, from some major event, or from some experience. The reason people don't get to their "something big" is that they don't identify what the real thing is and take a deep look at what has been holding them back—the obstacles.

Before we move into the next chapter, I want to leave you with a story and a question. It is a Cherokee legend, entitled, "Two Wolves."

"An old Cherokee is teaching his grandson about life. 'A fight is going on inside me,' he said to the boy. 'It is a terrible fight and it is between two wolves. One is evil—he is anger, envy, sorrow, regret, greed, arrogance, self-pity, guilt, resentment, inferiority, lies, false pride, superiority, and ego.' He continued, 'The other is good—he is joy, peace, love, hope, serenity, humility, kindness, benevolence, empathy, generosity, truth, compassion, and faith. The same fight is going on inside you—and inside every other person, too.'

∞

"The grandson thought about it for a minute and then asked his grandfather, 'Which wolf will win?'

"The old Cherokee simply replied, 'The one you feed.'"

As you consider going forward from here, think about what voice you are listening to and what voice will serve you best. It's your choice. Which one are you feeding? You have the power to change it. It's your choice. It's all up to you!

∞

What did you hear yourself saying when you wrote your letter?	Where did it come from?

∞

Old Story

New Story

∞

Infinite Epiphany

5

Setting Goals

"A dream is just a dream.
A goal is a dream with a plan and a deadline."
- Harvey Mackay

Congratulations on completing the exercises in the last chapter. Can you feel the power of actually putting things in writing? Do you now have more clarity about the obstacles that prevent you from moving in the direction of your vision? Have you uncovered obstacles that you may not have known existed?

Our obstacles, especially the ones we aren't able to identify, can be real sticking points to actualizing our vision. It's essential that we are able to see and acknowledge them. As soon as we do, we are already on our way to setting and achieving our goals. So, at this point, if you are still not clear about the actual obstacles that are preventing you from moving forward, I sug-

∞

gest that you go back to Chapter 4 and revisit the stories and beliefs that have been running in your life. I promise you that within those stories and beliefs lie the obstacles that keep you from your vision. The work in Chapter 4 is essential to what we are about to undertake in this chapter. If you feel you have a solid sense of the stories that have been running in your life, then it's time to move forward.

This is the moment in the process—the turning point—where you actually have the opportunity to activate a plan for your vision. It means that it is time to really put yourself into action, giving yourself a timeframe and (gasp!) possibly sharing it with others, which will help to hold yourself accountable.

This is where we separate the *men from the boys*—or *"women from the girls"*—so to speak. This is where you get to find out whether you are a dreamer or a doer—to discover which group you fall into. Dreamers can easily write down a dream and do nothing with it. Successful, living-in-financial-abundance, and enjoying-life-to-the-fullest people are not just dreamers; they are visionaries who are also doers. They keep their eye on the horizon, which is their vision. As they do so, they continue to move forward, holding their heads up each and every day as they work to bring their vision into reality.

Many individuals go through my workshops and when they get to this point, they freeze. It can be especially tough for people

∞

who have big issues that they've never addressed in their lives. By this time, we have often hit nerves that are painful and maybe even scary. It can be scary to look at what's inside, because once we do, change is required. Depending on how big the event or how deep the patterns and beliefs, this is where individuals have to decide whether to keep going or shut down. The choice is always ours.

Since most people use time and money to validate why their vision is not happening, rather than owning their story and taking brave steps to change their beliefs, it can be difficult to make that choice and declare that we're going to work on ourselves. It can be a challenge to go against the flow of what most people do—making excuses and believing that everything is outside of themselves rather than taking responsibility for what is happening in their lives.

I encourage you to courageously take those steps and keep going. Don't let your fears or the big issues prevent you from moving forward. If you need to seek the help of someone, please do so. Whether that is a trusted friend, colleague, mentor, coach, counselor, or even a family member who will give you the space and safety to be vulnerable and open, seek out their assistance.

Once you are fully committed and willing to do the work necessary to remove the obstacles, you are ready to start setting goals. This is where the real magic begins. This is where life can

∞

start to look different. And this is where we begin to move in the direction of our vision and our dreams.

There are thousands of books on goal-setting. After working with many different methods, I have created what I believe is an approach that combines the best of the best. With the following tools, you have the opportunity to take a very big vision and work at it in bite-size increments and watch it grow. This is where the "how" unfolds and your wings develop.

If you have ever done goal-setting work before, you've probably heard of, and even possibly worked with, S.M.A.R.T. goals. Here is the acronym and its meaning:

S = Specific, significant, stretching
M = Measurable, meaningful, motivational
A = Attainable, achievable, action-oriented
R = Realistic, results-oriented, relevant
T = Time-based, time-bound, trackable

There are several categories in life where you might choose to set goals. I group mine into the following five core life categories:

Faith/Community/Service—growing in your spiritual beliefs; serving in big or small ways; making a difference

Family/Relationships—structuring interactions, how time is spent and with whom it is spent

∞

Fitness/Health—tending to your physical well-being

Finance/Career—choosing what you do for a living; financial wealth

Foundation/Character—knowing who you are as a person, choosing traits to remove or improve; thinking about how others perceive you and talk about you

When you wrote your three-year vision, you used the above categories to create a lifestyle you envisioned for yourself in three years. As you move into goal-setting, it's essential that you are aware of and create a balance between your vision for your business and your vision for your life. What you envision for your lifestyle has to be supported by your business vision and vice versa. Sometimes, as people create their vision, they unknow-ingly include things professionally or personally that conflict with each other. For instance, if you want to live in Europe for part of the year, yet your business is located in a brick-and-mortar building somewhere in the United States, how will that work? Will you have someone manage your business for the time you are away, will you travel back and forth, or will you have weekly calls to ensure that everything is running the way you intended? Would another living arrangement closer to your business loca-tion provide you with what you envisioned for yourself by liv-ing in Europe? Or might it be time to consider another type of

∞

professional life that allows you to live in different geographic locations?

Here's another example. If you are the primary caretaker for aging parents in Colorado, yet your vision is to manage a bed and breakfast on the coast of Maine, is it possible to set goals and move in the direction of your professional vision at this time? If it is possible, what will your lifestyle and personal life need to look like in order to make that happen?

Our goals in each of the five categories must compliment and support each other. There needs to be a balance between them, taking into account where you are right now and where you want to go. It's essential to consider how they will "work" in concert with each other rather than unknowingly creating sets of goals that sabotage one another.

Also, as we move forward in this chapter, keep in mind the impact of goals in one category on another category. For example, if you set a Family Goal to travel twice a year, include the Financial Goal to fund it. If you set a Faith Goal to go on a mission trip with your church once a year, prepare to be physically fit and to have the finances to support you while you are away.

With these thoughts in mind, let's dive in. It's time to take your three-year vision (your ice cream scoop, which was further described in your three-year letter) and give it a foundation to rest upon ... your cone. You'll find a graphic of a cone for you to work with on the following page.

The first line down from your three-year vision "scoop" repre-

∞

sents your one-year goal mark. The next line down in the middle of the cone is six months. The line before you get to the tip of the cone is for your ninety-day goals. The very tip of your cone delineates your monthly-down-to-weekly action steps needed to keep you moving forward and producing results.

From now on, you can use this visual to live your life. This graphic helps you see and intentionally create the activities that line you up with your vision. Without attacking the tip of the cone with daily "to-do" lists that don't propel you in the direction of your vision, you can create goals that move you in the direction of your dreams.

Most people work in the reverse direction of the cone. They chip away at their daily to-do list, not considering whether or not those tasks line up with where they want to go. Before they know it, there is a big hole at the bottom of the cone and they've created a mess. They become so focused on the mess that they forget where they were going—towards that luscious ice cream vision at the top. And without being aware of what's happening, they find that their vision has melted away.

So, we have to start with the vision. Then as we work our way down the cone, we ask ourselves at each incremental step, "What goals do I need to set here (one year, six months, ninety days, monthly) to move me towards the next point in time?" In this way, we are continually working our goals in alignment with our vision.

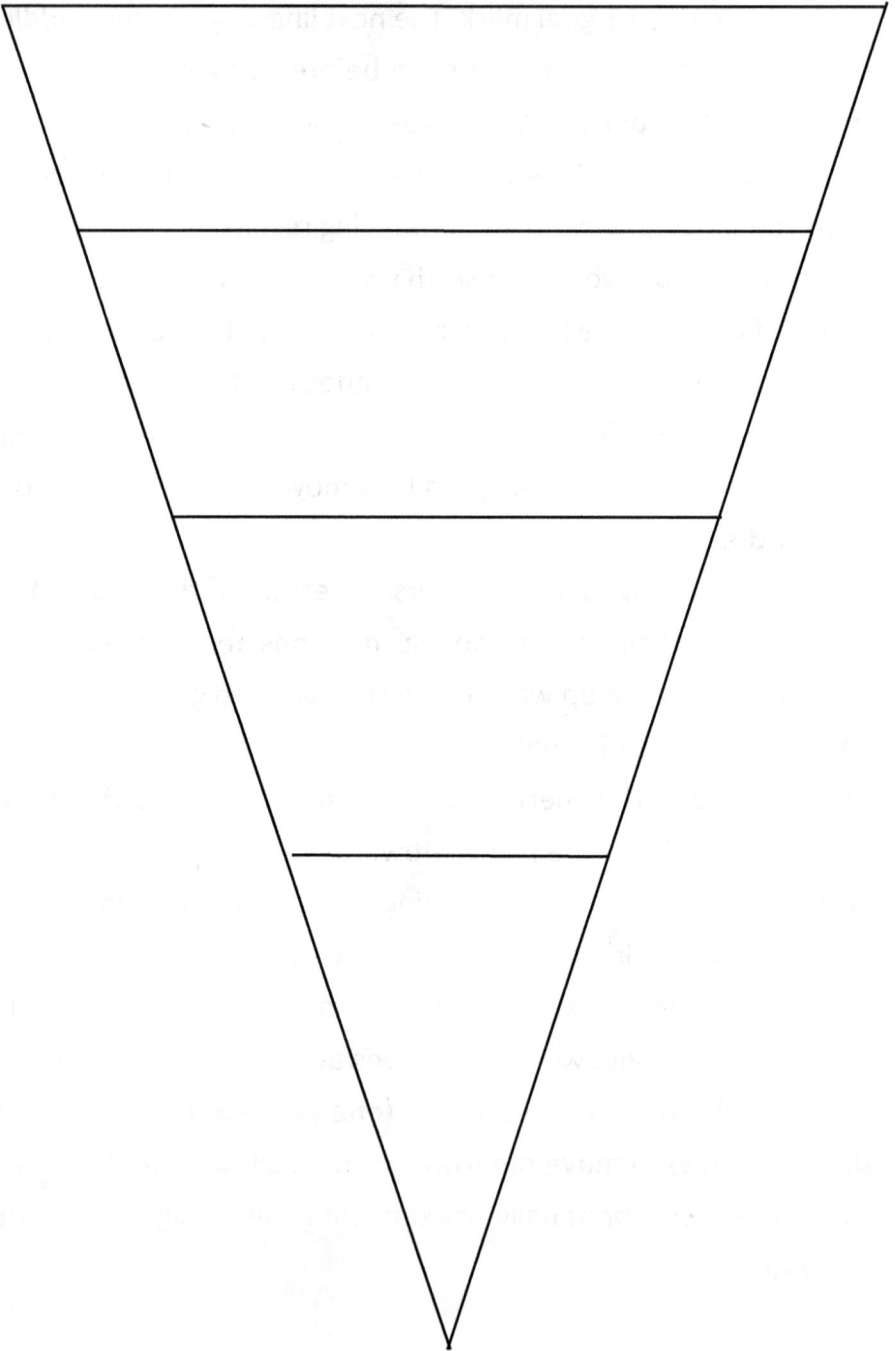

∞

∞

S.M.A.R.T. Goals

For the purpose of the following exercise, we won't focus on three-year goals. Since three years can seem so far away, it's much easier to set one-year goals and then set new ones at the end of each subsequent year.

Before you begin to create your own goals to support your three-year vision, let's walk through an example. In a workshop, I may ask someone to shout out a one-year goal they have in the category of Fitness/Health, and it usually sounds something like this: "I *want* to lose weight and feel better."

I then ask that we break down their one-year goal and test it to evaluate whether it is a S.M.A.R.T. goal or simply a dream. Using the words, "I want," "I hope," or "I am trying" are not specific. Everybody *wants* to be more fit, to have *more time* with family, or to possess *more money* in the bank, but these are not the basis for an action plan. They are not measurable. We cannot conclude whether the goal of losing weight and feeling better is Achievable or Realistic because we have not defined a measurement or a quantitative number as a target. And, despite stating this as what they want to achieve one year from now, a S.M.A.R.T. goal needs a specific date: with the month, date, and year.

So, a written S.M.A.R.T goal related to weight loss might look like this: "I *am* ten pounds lighter on December 31, 2016." This

∞

goal is specific. It tells us exactly how much lighter the person will be and by what date. It is measurable. Again, it gives us a number to achieve. Is it achievable? For the majority of people, losing ten pounds in a year is an achievable goal. Is it realistic? If the person has a health condition that makes weight loss extremely difficult, this may be an unrealistic goal. They may need to include a longer timeframe to make it achievable and realistic. For most of us, however, this is a realistic goal. Finally, is it time-based and trackable? Absolutely! Especially if the individual owns a scale or goes to the gym regularly, they will be able to track their progress. So, based on how this goal was written, it is a S.M.A.R.T. goal. Words matter!

One last comment about creating goals. Notice that this goal starts out with the words, "I am." Goals that begin with, "I am," "I will," "I did," or some other phrase that denotes clear intention are powerful. They are action-oriented and active rather than passive. They are clear rather than wishy-washy, and that makes them truly possible and achievable.

Now it's your turn. Use the goal sheets on the following pages to delineate your goals for each time frame, filling in a S.M.A.R.T. goal in each of the five main categories. I've provided multiple copies of the goal sheet so you can use some now and keep at least one as a blank master for the future. You can also copy the information from the goal sheet into your notebook or journal and record your goals there.

∞

Be sure to look back at the definitions from the beginning of this chapter as you write each one. Once you've created a goal in each category, look at them again and consider whether they are balanced. Will they support each other rather than cause conflict or cancel each other out?

∞

Goals for _____

(1 year, 6 months, 90 days, 1 month, 1 week)

S = Smart M = Measurable A = Attainable R = Realistic T = Time-Bound

For each goal, list specific/measurable/dated activities to overcome the obstacle and meet the goal.

Goal: _____ Obstacle: _____

_____

_____

_____

Goal: _____ Obstacle: _____

_____

_____

_____

Goal: _____ Obstacle: _____

_____

_____

_____

Goal: _____ Obstacle: _____

_____

_____

_____

∞

Goals for _____
(1 year, 6 months, 90 days, 1 month, 1 week)

S = Smart M = Measurable A = Attainable R = Realistic T = Time-Bound

For each goal, list specific/measurable/dated activities to overcome the obstacle and meet the goal.

Goal: _____ Obstacle: _____
_____
_____
_____

Goal: _____ Obstacle: _____
_____
_____
_____

Goal: _____ Obstacle: _____
_____
_____
_____

Goal: _____ Obstacle: _____
_____
_____
_____

∞

Goals for _____

(1 year, 6 months, 90 days, 1 month, 1 week)

S = Smart M = Measurable A = Attainable R = Realistic T = Time-Bound

For each goal, list specific/measurable/dated activities to overcome the obstacle and meet the goal.

Goal: _____ Obstacle: _____

_____

_____

_____

Goal: _____ Obstacle: _____

- -

- -

- -

- -

Goal: _____ Obstacle: _____

_____

_____

_____

Goal: _____ Obstacle: _____

_____

_____

_____

∞

Goals for _____

(1 year, 6 months, 90 days, 1 month, 1 week)

S = Smart M = Measurable A = Attainable R = Realistic T = Time-Bound

For each goal, list specific/measurable/dated activities to overcome the obstacle and meet the goal.

Goal: _____ Obstacle: _____

_____

_____

_____

Goal: _____ Obstacle: _____

- -

- -

- -

Goal: _____ Obstacle: _____

_____

_____

_____

Goal: _____ Obstacle: _____

_____

_____

_____

∞

Goals for _____

(1 year, 6 months, 90 days, 1 month, 1 week)

S = Smart M = Measurable A = Attainable R = Realistic T = Time-Bound

For each goal, list specific/measurable/dated activities to overcome the obstacle and meet the goal.

Goal: _____ Obstacle: _____

_____

_____

_____

Goal: _____ Obstacle: _____

_____

_____

_____

Goal: _____ Obstacle: _____

_____

_____

_____

Goal: _____ Obstacle: _____

_____

_____

_____

∞

Goals for _____

(1 year, 6 months, 90 days, 1 month, 1 week)

S = Smart M = Measurable A = Attainable R = Realistic T = Time-Bound

For each goal, list specific/measurable/dated activities to overcome the obstacle and meet the goal.

Goal: _____ Obstacle: _____

_____

_____

_____

Goal: _____ Obstacle: _____

_____

_____

_____

Goal: _____ Obstacle: _____

_____

_____

_____

Goal: _____ Obstacle: _____

_____

_____

_____

∞

If you have put some serious thought into your goals, your heart may be pumping a little faster right now. When moving in the direction of your vision starts to get real as a result of setting goals, those voices make themselves known: "Pshaww! You've done this before and it didn't work." "You always say you are going to get fit and you never do." "You don't have the education or skills to achieve that career."

The invisible wall goes up brutally fast to block the goal and your efforts to achieve it. In order to move forward, you have to scale that wall first. Unfortunately, the "wall" is never stated as one of the typical reasons people say they can't achieve the goal. The "wall" is most often a *real* obstacle.

As I mentioned earlier, time and money are the two biggest excuses people give themselves for not achieving goals. It is simply because, as a culture, we continually justify those excuses. "Everyone else uses them too." This is what most people say to validate each other's and their own excuses. Instead of encouraging each other to move beyond these excuses, we all look at one another with the expectation to maintain the status quo. It's comfortable, so we want to nestle there and we want others to stay there with us. It's hard to see other people succeed when we're stuck. It feels better if we're all miserable, because at least we're all in it together.

The good news is that my intention is to not let that happen to

∞

you. So, it's time to test your goals and identify the potential *real* obstacles. Take a look at each goal and consider the obstacles you identified in the previous chapter. Are there obstacles—stories or beliefs—that might prevent you from accomplishing your goal or that might need to be further addressed before you can be successful? Remember that these are the real obstacles that could get in your way rather than the circumstances you've used in the past to explain why you couldn't achieve a particular goal.

Let's go back to our weight loss example for a moment. We identified a S.M.A.R.T. goal: *I am ten pounds lighter on December 31, 2016.* In my workshops, at this point I ask, "So if this is your goal, what is the biggest obstacle that could prevent you from accomplishing it?" The individual may reply, "I don't have the time or money to join a gym." I then ask, "Can we all agree as a group that there are people who lose ten pounds without joining a gym?" After the group and the individual agree that this is true, we then dig deeper. I will ask, "Since we all have agreed that it is not time or money, and a gym membership is not necessary to lose ten pounds, let's go back to your stories. Are any of those stories related to this obstacle?" The individual may then respond, "I'm thinking that I have the belief that I can't really lose the weight because nobody in my family has ever done that before."

That awareness unlocks the mystery of why this goal has not been achieved up to now. For some people, it can be an even big-

∞

ger issue. Maybe from the time they were small, they were told they'd always be bigger than others. Maybe they were told that everyone in their family is big-boned and they are too.

Once we've uncovered the *real* obstacle, we can begin to set baby step activities to tackle that obstacle. At this point in my workshops, I ask what three action steps could the individual take to attack that obstacle. The action steps must address the obstacle rather than the goal. If we do not take steps to change the belief, no matter what steps we may take towards the goal— hire a personal trainer, hire a nutritionist, walk for thirty minutes every day, etc.—we will not achieve it. The baby steps, the actions to put in place, must be directed at changing the belief. In order to change deep-seated beliefs, a complete mind shift is necessary.

So, in our example, the individual might then take two hours each week and research online to find other people who have achieved this goal. She might research and read stories written by others who have lost weight even when their families were large. The person might read blogs and articles of inspiration to build positive personal affirmations or she might begin to listen to recordings that are designed to break down messaging that doesn't serve her. She could also join a Meetup group with others who are working on the same issues. She might seek the help of a professional, such as a counselor or life coach, or she might

∞

reach out to another person who has been successful and find out how they did it.

The key is that the individual is now able to walk away from something that looks monumental, or even impossible to achieve, and they are excited because they have identified baby steps to help them break down the obstacle. That already puts them on their path to achieving what they want.

The key here is to acknowledge the real obstacles so we can begin to eliminate them and move in the direction of our goals.

As with the example we looked at in this chapter, when someone can't seem to lose weight and says it's because of time and money, we have to get to the deeper underlying beliefs and stories. The clue that they exist reveals itself by looking at what others are able to do. How can we ignore people who have busier lives than we do, yet who manage to stay physically fit? They *make* time to work out and eat healthier. We also know people who stay fit without the expense of a gym or personal trainer. There are plenty of ways to exercise without spending money. Hmmm! It's easy to rationalize our excuses. It can feel safer to keep those *real* obstacles hidden away.

Whenever you come up to resistance or the inability to move in the direction of a goal, it's important to revisit the "stories" from your history that sabotaged your self-confidence. Consider whether you've allowed those stories to become your "beliefs"

∞

rather than dismissing them as "stories" from your past.

When I dig a little deeper with people about including their obstacle/wall/stories on their goals document, we usually uncover the core of the problem that might sound something like the following:

"I don't believe I can really do it."

"No one in my family ever exercised so I don't believe I should have to."

"I am uncomfortable/embarrassed to exercise in front of other people."

"I'm not self-motivated."

When you understand the real obstacles, you have the ammunition to break down that wall to get to your goal. Victory starts with baby-step actions. If lack of belief that you can do it is a blocker, include action steps to change that. Use the three lines following the goal on your goal sheet to address that issue if you can't chase it away yourself. For example, physically write down those baby-step actions:

"I will read books about people who struggled to lose weight and learn how they finally did it, for inspiration and to change my belief."

"I will display some pictures of *myself* when I was the weight I intend to be to rebuild that vision of myself."

"I will seek out other people who are doing things I enjoy by

∞

joining a walking group in the neighborhood, or a hiking club, or a dance class, etc."

These smaller, daily action steps can be a foundation for your monthly, ninety-day, six-month, and one-year goals.

Any steps you take and commit to is success.

The only way you fail in life is to do nothing at all.

Goal-setting is a learned skill. Give yourself time to write your goals and know that you will get better and better at it.

Infinite Epiphany

6

Becoming a True Leader

*"Great leaders don't blame the tools they are given,
they work to sharpen them."*
- Simon Sinek

When I use the word "leadership" in a workshop I can almost feel the air go out of people. They start squirming in their seats, the look of hope from seeing their vision starts to fade, and some appear flat out terrified. There are many, many misperceptions about leadership that create these feelings.

Leadership is really about becoming a person of integrity and character and about having the willingness to lead yourself in order to then lead others. Leadership means you understand that who you become in the process is even bigger than the skills you learn. You have to be willing to change, to be adaptable, flexible, vulnerable, and transparent. A leader cannot get to the

∞

big visions without having a team, and that requires that you be willing to take a look at yourself in the mirror. Most people don't go here because it requires internal changes more than external learning. The idea of being a leader scares most people to death, so they don't go beyond what they can do independently.

When I ask groups, "If we can all agree that leadership is a must, what gets in the way of being a leader?" their responses include statements like, "Leaders have to babysit people," "Leaders have to be perfect," and "Leaders have to be 'on' 24/7." People have all sorts of fallacies about what it means to be a leader. I'm here to tell you that leaders are not perfect and they aren't on 24/7. They've simply learned how to put boundaries around their time and around who they spend it with. Leaders lead by example and they mentor. Leaders have to be willing to continuously work on themselves. When leaders have a plan, people will follow.

Integrity shows up in a true leader by the way they do the right thing whether people are watching or not. Leaders are congruent in their character—they don't paint a pretty picture on the outside and then live in a completely different way. Leaders are congruent in all aspects of their lives, whether they're in the public's eye or not. They live the way they say they live. Leaders never posture themselves as being all together or perfect. They are transparent about their journey. The more they can

∞

share what they're going through or what they've been through, the more people are able to relate to them—people are able to believe what they say and want to follow that person.

Here's an example. I cry on stage, and I tell people I hate that I do it. The way I cry is actually sobbing—it's breath-taking-away crying. People tell me they love when it happens because it's real and they can connect to me. I honestly would like to stop crying so intensely when I share parts of myself, but at this point I have to accept that *it is what it is.*

Here's another example. About ten years ago, I made a horrible personal mistake. I had to tell my team what had happened, because we were about to spend time together. Apparently, up to this point they believed I had it all together and never made mistakes. After I told them about the mistake, they all expressed how relieved they were to find out I didn't walk on water.

Good leaders are transparent and congruent in their journey to strive to be better. A leader's motto needs to be, "Strive for excellence rather than perfection."

By now, you may have started to see a common thread running through what this really all comes down to in order to succeed. There are countless reasons why even with all the best training on the subject of vision and goals people still do not go after their dreams. With the hundreds of people I have coached over the years, I can honestly tell you that when you peel the onion all the way to the core it comes down to this—YOU have to want to change and grow.

To create your vision, you have to be willing to let go of the past, to forgive whoever you feel has wronged you, to stop holding onto events that have created those stories, to make some changes in your routine and who your spend your time with, and most of all, to start working on growing into the person who has always been inside. You have to choose to become a leader.

You also have to grow into your goals. We all need time to grow into the next level. Most people know that being the person they are today, they aren't prepared to handle as big of a dream as their vision represents. So what has to happen alongside growing into your goals, and ultimately your vision, is doing the work to personally grow into that person who can handle a business and a lifestyle on a much bigger level.

We all have personal things we have to change in order to be the person who can handle the dream. We all have to go to work. We have to learn from those who have already gotten there, we have to be willing to be super-coachable, and we have to be willing to be completely vulnerable to hear the tough stuff about ourselves.

Unlike people who are willing to grow into their goals and vision, when what I call "gap" people write their three-year vision, they become unwilling to do the work necessary to move

∞

in the direction of what they desire. They are unable to see how it could possibly happen RIGHT NOW based on their current circumstances and their current skill level. We all come to that fork in the road, understanding that we need a vision and goals, and we need to be intentional about what we're doing to move in that direction. Because of where "gap" people are in their personal internal work, education, family situation, lifestyle, and more, it's hard for them to wrap their head around the dream. Those current factors become great big obstacles.

We need to understand that there will be gaps. There will be things we have to work on. We may need to go back to school, to build skills alongside a current full-time job. We may need to give up time-wasting activities, such as watching TV or hanging out late at night with friends. For some people, that gap is so big, it becomes overwhelming. The biggest gap of all is usually the internal shifts that are required.

As we've looked at in a number of ways, it comes down to our ability to know that the first thing we have to decide to do is work internally in order to make changes. We have to commit to the change that is necessary. We must have a willingness to commit as well as an ability to trust and have faith that we're going to get there. For "gap" people, this is difficult. They doubt they can make those internal changes. They doubt themselves. Unfortunately, most people retreat when they figure out they

∞

have to make some internal changes to habits and their behavior. But when people become willing to give it a try, things begin to shift. As they change, their confidence increases. As baby step shifts occur, their confidence grows even more, which gives them the self-motivation to keep going.

People always have a choice. Some people humble themselves and admit that there are things they need to work on. They then go to work on those areas. Others say that the process is too hard and they retreat. Most "gap" people don't even own up to their belief that they can't do it. They simply disappear. They vaporize back into their current lives.

The good news is that our vision doesn't happen overnight. It's not meant to happen overnight. Sometimes when we jump in too fast, before we're ready or have the support we need or the self-awareness, self-development, and skills, it can implode on us. However, little by little, with consistent, focused work, you can absolutely become the person to manage your dream and your vision. You have to grow into your vision, and that takes time. Everything we gather as we grow is for a purpose to be used later. All that we acquire helps us build strength, confidence, and the knowing of what we're doing and what we're moving towards. If we choose to see that everything is for our highest purpose, it's easy to be patient and trust the process as it unfolds.

It truly requires eighty percent character and twenty per-

∞

cent skill to be a leader. Unfortunately, this mix becomes the stopping point for most people. Are you someone who doesn't like change? I hate to tell you this, but I have seen many of the people I work with come to this point of doing the internal work that's necessary to support their vision, and right when they get so close they can almost touch their dream, they retreat. People who are not willing to be transparent, vulnerable, authentic, or able to share in community with others about what is going on in their lives often come to a dead halt at this point.

As you consider where you'll go from here, I invite you to look at what your motivations are—are you moaning and whining and wanting people to say "poor you" or are you looking for help to lift you up? We can either amplify where we're at or move forward. Those who retreat go back to settling for the life and the job that does not fulfill them, telling themselves that it's okay.

I have gotten used to many disappointments in my career, but I will never stop feeling sad when I see someone who has every-thing in them—the potential and skills, the support through their family and friends—not go after their dream. When they get to the place where they need to make the internal changes for themselves and their families, they become paralyzed. As much as I strive to help them see their potential, there are individuals who won't unfreeze and move through the journey they need to experience in order to move in the direction of their dreams.

∞

I will never get used to watching someone walk away from their incredible potential and possibility.

The secret ingredient in the ones who do move towards their dreams is the size of the vision they hold. They're the ones who want that vision so bad in their life that they cannot think of breathing without it. They want it like the air they need to survive. I have seen people with major obstacles, including health issues, a lack of skills, outside responsibilities, and more, go for it. They want it so bad that they're willing to go through whatever it takes to get there.

There's a big difference between having a desire for something and feeling like they're suffocating if they don't do it. True leaders live and breathe their vision 24/7. Their creative process is active 24/7. They are always in creation mode. They can't shut it off. They dream about their vision every single night. So when someone says they want something, I ask them to tell me about what they want. If they can't repeat what they wanted three days later, it's a big clue to me that they don't really have a clear vision and they're not really committed to it.

If something is "the thing," you won't be able to resist it. If you are resisting, it's either not the thing or you're not ready to commit and do the work. If you find that you keep getting off track, I suggest that one day you write a little note and put it on the refrigerator and say, "I don't want it that bad and it's okay."

∞

It's hard to admit when people don't want something, so most people vaporize when they come to that realization. Because they feel a sense of shame, as if they're letting others down—including their coaches—they disappear.

When you come to that fork in the road in your own life, you get to choose. You can either choose to follow the norm or to be the leader of your life. Remember, leadership is never about being absolutely perfect in order to lead. This will NEVER happen! Just like I mentioned at the beginning of this chapter, I can imagine what you might be thinking about yourself right now: "I have too many faults"; "What if people find out I am really a mess?"; "People don't know all the mistakes I've made"; "I have never been a good leader"; "I am going to have to manage people and I can't even manage myself!" Yet, it's very simple. Just like everything else in this book, we make a discovery and go to work to improve it. To help you go to work, I've created a list of traits that successful leaders have developed. I am choosing that word "developed" specifically because these are skills that can be learned and improved. More good news!

Without attaching any judgment (just like when you wrote your stories) take some time to rank yourself from 1 to 10 (10 being the best) on how you feel you are doing right now in these areas. I have provided questions to help you understand how these traits/characteristics might show up. These questions are meant to provide clues to the following characteristics and traits.

∞

Vision & Belief

Do you have a written, specific vision statement for your life and/or your business? Can you articulate it clearly to other people? Do you say it with belief and confidence?

Perspective & Attitude

How do you view life overall? When you talk to people do you usually talk about everything that is wrong in your life, or about all the new things you are excited to create? Do you choose to see the good in every situation?

Goal Setting

Have you broken your vision down into those bite-size goals? Do you work on them regularly to stay on track or readjust if and when needed?

Courage & Determination

Are you willing to face the fear and do it anyway?

Willingness to Be a Team Player

Do you have a "what's in it for me?" attitude or are you always thinking, "How can I show up to be of some value to others even if I don't feel like it?"

∞

Self-Motivation

Are you able to keep working on your goals even when you are working alone, or do you only get into activity when other people are pushing you?

Consistency

Do you stay plugged into your daily intentional activity to achieve the goals, show up where/when to what you said you were committed to, or do you float in and out?

Coachable

Do you seek out advice from successful mentors and really listen to what they are telling you without getting defensive? Do you apply what they tell you even if it's humbling or uncomfortable?

Focused

Can you stay on one task at a time? Do you apply intentional activities every ninety days that you know will move you forward and avoid "ping ponging" all over the place?

Time Management

Do you have a good handle on blocking your time to stay focused on those intentional activities?

∞

Money Management

Do you have a good relationship with money and do you treat it with respect? Do you have a responsible plan for how to create and invest your money wisely?

Organization

Do you have a work space that is neat and easy to work in, or do you have to spend too much time moving things around, hunting for things you can't find, and losing time doing it?

Reliable

Do you do what you say you are going to do? Do you show up consistently or do people have to always wonder what you are up to? Can people trust you?

Communicative

Do you communicate your intentions with others? Do you follow through and say the things that need to be said in a way that is clear and professional?

Manage Emotion/Words/Actions

Can you separate whatever immediate emotion you are having from the task at hand? Can you keep an emotion in a proper

∞

perspective and not allow it to filter into your communication and stay focused on the activity? (One of the BIGGEST gifts of a true leader is learning how to manage emotions!)

Boundaries

Do you have clear boundaries around your time, your space, and most especially, WHO you share it with? Can you protect and value yourself enough to choose only people and activities that add value to who you are and where you are going?

My guess is that you scored pretty well in some of these areas because you either come by them naturally or you have developed the skill somewhere along the way. For instance, some people love time structure and follow time well, while others have more of a free spirit and a difficult time committing to time structure. They'd rather float through the day. Scientifically, those people can't feel time passing. If those in the latter group have identified that time structure is difficult and want to improve, they may have incorporated tools that help them manage their time.

You probably also saw some areas that could use some improvement in your life. Again, the choice is yours; you either go to work to learn the skills and tools to support the characteristics you inherently have, or to become a habit that creates a new

∞

characteristic, or to strengthen one that is already a part of you. If you don't, eventually you will stall out your growth or plateau until you're ready to build the new supporting skills. These are true characteristics of leadership—somebody who has chosen to build their own dream and follow their own path and become really good at it.

Remember that you are not going for perfection. You will always have some areas that are going to be more challenging than others, but keep working on them.

Each of these areas can be improved upon by reading the right books, attending workshops, working with tools, experts, and coaches, and applying what you learn consciously every day, which leads to a change in your daily habits. The BEST way I have personally learned these skills has been by being around amazing people who have modeled it for me as well as through seeking out mentors in my life.

You have another choice to consider as well—you can choose to keep doing things the hard way (doing it ineffectively first and then having to change course afterwards), or having someone in your life who has "been there, done that," whether it's someone in your chosen field or not. And this is where having a coach or mentor comes in.

I have become a true believer that mentorship and coaching is everything. The number one thing that every single person

∞

needs in life is a coach. Because what they do is tell you where you're at right now and point out that if you keep going you'll end up in this place down the road. As a coach, I can see further out than my clients. That helps them change course and avoid the pitfalls so they don't have to take the harder road. When someone gets off course it can cost a person way more time and money than they'll invest to work with a coach. Once more, the choice is always ultimately yours.

Infinite Epiphany

Conclusion

"As long as you are alive, you will either live to accomplish your own goals and dreams or be used as a resource to accomplish someone else's."
- Grant Cardone

It all comes down to choices. You either make the choice to follow your own path in life, to be brave, and make the hard changes, to follow your dreams, or you continue to follow the path others have set for you.

When I ask people who choose the latter whether or not they feel fulfilled, they tell me that they are not. They go to a job they don't love, they hang with people who are stagnant, they follow what they've been told to do. Most people are really not okay with the latter. This is why most people are depressed, sick, and constantly compare themselves to others.

I think the worst thing that can happen for a person is to die

∞

with regret, thinking they could have done better for themselves, their families, their communities. Making statements such as, "If only I had..."

You have the choice to live a fulfilling life. You can choose a life of intention and big vision that goes beyond yourself and extends into the world and into future generations.

That little voice inside you was put there for a reason. I truly believe God has a purpose for each and every one of us. If each of us comes to realize our purpose, doing what we were sent here to do, it will truly be heaven on earth.

My ultimate goal in life is to help people get back to that little voice. I believe it will be a whole different world when we do.

I'd like to leave you with a beautiful quote from George Bernard Shaw. The words summarize what I hope for you and your life:

> *"This is the true joy in life, being used for a purpose recognized by yourself as a mighty one. Being a force of nature instead of a feverish, selfish little clod of ailments and grievances complaining that the world will not devote itself to making you happy. I am of the opinion that my life belongs to the whole community and as I live it is my privilege - my privilege to do for it whatever I*

∞

can. I want to be thoroughly used up when I die, for the harder I work the more I love. I rejoice in life for its own sake. Life is no brief candle to me; it is a sort of splendid torch which I've got a hold of for the moment and I want to make it burn as brightly as possible before handing it on to future generations."

- George Bernard Shaw

Gratitude and Acknowledgments

Everything I know and teach comes from the outpouring of mentorship, encouragements, and love from the people who have always seen my greatness and willingly given me their valuable time and priceless advice.

To Penny Brendan, whose beautiful mind helped put the victory in my vision. Nédra Jané, thank you for being the first person to tell me I was on the wrong path and to see something greater in me than following the status quo. Because of the seeds you unknowingly planted within me, my life's vision became clear. That clarity has helped me help others—thousands of people who've become clear about their own vision and purpose.

Rita Davenport, you have been, and continue to be, my great-

∞

est source of inspiration, motivation, and personal and professional growth in my life. I am honored to call you my friend and my sweet "Mama Rita."

Keith Kochner, I am so thankful that God put you in my life exactly when I needed you as a mentor. You helped me navigate a very difficult time in my life and career, and I thank you for continuing to guide me forward.

Dr. Shad Helmstetter, thank you for teaching me and thousands of others how to change those damaging thoughts into positive voices to create the life of our dreams. I will always be grateful for you encouraging me to become a speaker and coach.

Thank you to all of the amazing leaders in Arbonne who paved the path for women and men to become the best they can be, and most especially the endless hours of coaching and love you gave me to become who I am today. Everything I pass on now to the people whom I coach is mostly the love, advice, and things I gleaned from watching and being around all of you. Your greatness rubbed off and I am forever grateful.

Thank you to my parents and family who had the hardest job of all—raising me. I love you and thank you for your patience, discipline (Lord knows I needed it!), and encouragement.

My family extends to my closest and dearest friends who have stuck by me through the some of the darkest days of my life and loved me anyway: Dawn Koenig, Angie Austin, Angel and Jay

∞

Tuccy, Eric Reamer, Tony Raburn, Penny and Kent Brenden, Anne Kocur, and Natalie Lewis. I am so happy to be serving people alongside all of you, and having a LOT of fun doing it!

To ALL of the people who I have had the honor to coach, I THANK YOU in a very big way. It is truly a blessing to watch you grow into YOUR greatness and courageously go after your dreams. You inspire me and make me better every day.

Lastly, to the people who are to come into my path in the present and future, I thank you. Our community only grows by welcoming in the amazing people out there who not only want to add value to their own lives, but are willing to create something bigger together.

Carey Conley's life changing Vision is *Victory* lessons are best learned from Carey herself.

CAREY CONLEY is a speaker and entrepreneurial coach specializing in creating a clear, concise vision for her clients' businesses and lives. She is also a weekly contributor to a number of nationally syndicated radio shows.

As co-creator of the inspired community, Infinite Nation, she believes success is about following your true passion. The purpose and mission of Infine Nation is to provide guidance, vision mentoring, proven training, and to support entrepreneurs at all levels to achieve success.

Contact Carey to Create a Vision for Your Life and Business
∞ **www.InfiniteNation.com** ∞

"I not only learned the skills needed to take my business to the next level, but found being part of the Infinite Nation community was invaluable!"
- Donna Galassi | President, Blue Zenith Web Design

"Carey's coaching and programs have contributed to a 200% increase in revenue annually."
- Katie Myers | CEO, CR Conversations

"Since hiring Carey Conley 9 months ago my business income has increased by 47.2 %. My company hired additional staff to accommodate growth."
- Kimbirly Orr | President, Knock Out Performance

"I left a job for a shoe-string idea to start a business, but working with Carey's Infinite Nation, I created a vision. I now have a thriving business and have learned more than I did during 8 years of education and 10 years in the workforce."
- Phylecia Jones | CFO & Founder, Keep Up with Mrs. Jones

www.ingramcontent.com/pod-product-compliance
Lightning Source LLC
Chambersburg PA
CBHW071856200326
41519CB00016B/4405